Literary Capital and
the Late Victorian Novel

Literary Capital and
the Late Victorian Novel

N. N. Feltes

THE UNIVERSITY OF WISCONSIN PRESS

The University of Wisconsin Press
114 North Murray Street
Madison, Wisconsin 53715

3 Henrietta Street
London, WC2E 8LU, England

1   2   3   4   5

Printed in the United States of America

Library of Congress Cataloging-in-Publication Data
Feltes, N. N. (Norman N.)
    Literary capital and the late Victorian novel / N. N. Feltes
        186 p.   cm.
        Includes bibliographical references and index.
        ISBN 0-299-13660-4   ISBN 0-299-13664-7 (pbk.)
        1. English fiction—19th century—History and criticism.
    2. Capitalism and literature—Great Britain—History—19th century.
    3. Literature and society—Great Britain—History—19th century.
    4. Authors and publishers—Great Britain—History—19th century.
    5. Literature publishing—Great Britain—History—19th century.
    6. Fiction—Authorship—Economic aspects—Great Britain.
    7. Great Britain—Economic conditions—19th century.
    I. Title.
PR878.C25F44   1993
823'.809358—dc20   92-35455

To George Wotton and Paul O'Flinn

If "Marx's path" is an example to us, it is not because of his origins and circumstances but because of his ferocious insistence on freeing himself from the myths which presented themselves as the *truth*, and because of the role of the experience of real history which elbowed these myths aside.

Louis Althusser, "On the Young Marx"

Contents

Preface

MY title is not a pun. This book is about "literary capital" in England at the end of the nineteenth century in its widest manifestations, for instance, in the textual ideology of the novels I examine in the last two chapters. But before that, the book attempts to rethink late Victorian publishing as literary capital, as a distinct historical formation within late Victorian capitalism. I develop the contention of my *Modes of Production of Victorian Novels* (1986) that British publishing transformed itself over the course of the nineteenth century from a petty-commodity literary mode of production to a capitalist literary mode of production (here I specify that it is a *patriarchal*/capitalist literary mode of production). Most particularly, and finally, this transformation was marked by the replacement in the nineties of the dominant structure of lending libraries/three-volume format/high initial price/delayed reprinting, by the single-volume, cheap format and the Net Book Agreement. It is in this new structure of trading arrangements that "publishing," as a distinctively capitalist organization of book production, comes into its own historically and is to be understood theoretically. This understanding, of course, sharply distinguishes this book from earlier studies of Victorian readers and their books, the Victorian novel and the reading public, publishers and publishing, and social histories of the late Victorian novel. None of the earlier studies are interested in late Victorian capital as a determining structure, and perhaps because of this, none question sufficiently the historical status of their "facts," whether institutions, events, or texts. I try to do that, to read these materials "symptomatically," as related parts of a structured totality I call, first, "literary capital," and then, "publishing."

Late Victorian literary capital is a structured totality, but it is also a process. Not only does it have its own particular processes of accumulation, of making profits, but these processes are themselves in process, and I try to bear that in mind and to show these processes as contradictory and changing. While my first chapter attempts to map out synchronically the structures of late Victorian publishing, it concludes by locating a primary contradiction in the relation between what I call "list" and "entrepreneurial" publishing practices. The second chapter addresses the social construction of various late Victorian ideologies of literary value; again, while I am interested in the specifics of these instances, I try also to place them historically in the larger transformation of book production. In these chapters I want to have analyzed neither a static totality nor an unstructured agglomeration; my attempt is to do a dialectical analysis. The last two chapters, each situating three novels in a particular time, attempt also to analyze historical, ideological processes and are juxtaposed to indicate continuity and change.

I want, finally, to say a word about two other formal aspects of the book. First: *Literary Capital* has only four chapters, and they are quite long. I have give this format considerable thought and have concluded that a looser one would undercut my effort to present an analysis of a structured totality. In the Althusserian/Poulantzian tradition in which I am trying to work, one looks to the "levels" of a social formation rather than to the discrete categories of positivist social science. Each of my chapters determinedly explores a "level," sociopolitical or ideological, to find what can be known on that level. This question relates to the other formal aspect of the book which I want to mention. "Dialectical," "symptomatic," "totality" are examples of a technical language which I employ when I need to do so. This whole project is an attempt to bring marxist structuralist theory to bear on the empirical records of late Victorian novel production. "Any theoretical discourse," Althusser writes,

> has as its ultimate goal the knowledge of . . . particular concrete real objects; either their individuality (the structure of a social formation) or the modes of this individuality (the successive conjunctures in which this social formation *exists*).[1]

This is an admirably lucid statement of the knowledge I am seeking in this book (even of the formal arrangement I have been describing), and to approach that knowledge I must occasionally ensure that the theoretical framework is in place.

Without a doubt, this work is complexly overdetermined, made possible only by innumerable individuals and institutions, some of which I may be unaware of. However, I am very aware of many debts to specific institutions and to particular individuals. I am obligated to the Social Sciences and Humanities Research Council of Canada (and to the millions of Canadians who provide their funds) for a release-time grant which allowed me to spend 1990–91 working in the Bodleian Library, Oxford, and to York University (the same extension should be made) and the York University Faculty Association for a sabbatical leave in 1991–92 and a supplemental grant toward research expenses. I am grateful as well to Terry Eagleton for nominating me, and to the Master of Linacre College, Oxford, Sir Brian Cartledge, and the Fellows of Linacre College, for welcoming me as a Visiting Senior Member for 1990–91, to Carol Creed and Lynette Soanes at Linacre for assisting me, and to Dr. Peter Kilby for helping me to Linacre's computer facilities. Also, I am deeply indebted to Ann Edmunds of the Library of the Oxford Polytechnic for making possible my study of Walter Besant. In the Bodleian Library I was assisted daily by Tina King, Helen Rogers, and Vera Ryhajlo, and by Richard Bell. In Toronto, my greatest debt is to the staff of the Robarts Library of the University of Toronto, especially to Mary McTavish, and to the staff of the Scott Library, York University. I have been helped, as well, by the staff of the Newberry Library, Chicago, and the University of Michigan Library.

In the late winter of 1991, the library workers of the University of Toronto, Local 1230, Canadian Union of Public Employees, struck against the university administration. This is not the place to discuss the politics of that strike (except to express my total sympathy with the library workers), but I might mention that for three months their picket line (the Robarts Library remaining "open") closed to me the major research library in central Canada, elbowing aside, so to speak, my scholarly project. I owe them for some knowledge, but luckily for my project there were other resources, such as the fine collection of Victorian periodicals in the Metropolitan Toronto Central Reference Library; I am very grateful to their staff for their patience with my unusual requests. I want to thank also Mary Hudecki and Gladys Fung of the Scott

Library Interlibrary Loan Department for their generosity and skill in helping me locate alternative sources in southern Ontario. And I am grateful to the staff of the Mills Library, McMaster University, and the staff of the Porter Library, University of Waterloo.

Dr. Simon Eliot has read drafts of parts of the manuscript, and Professor John Goode and Professor Patricia Srebrnik have read a draft of the whole and have generously advised me. I am truly grateful for their considered comments, and I am only slightly less thankful to the numerous friends who have from time to time listened to a current problem and helped me through it. I am very aware of all this assistance, personal and institutional, that has converged on me during these months, and while I am most grateful, I recognize my own responsibility for what I have done with it, for the errors and faults remaining in *Literary Capital*.

Literary Capital and
the Late Victorian Novel

1. Publishing as Capital

THE materials available for a history of publishing at the turn of the century include trade journals, publishers' archives, histories of particular firms and biographies of publishers and authors, narrative accounts of the rise of publishing, general social histories of the time, and, more recently, histories of publishing itself. In this chapter I want to address these materials anew and, while making use of the wealth of empirical detail, nevertheless to avoid empiricism. I want to escape the illusion that their interpretation somehow lies in the materials themselves, in adding something new or reorganizing them in some new way, or in devising a new way of handling quantitatively intractable lists and account books, or in the simple sequence of books. I have tried here to replace these various empiricist approaches with a marxist structuralist problematic. In the "Theses on Feuerbach," Marx wrote:

> the chief defect of all hitherto existing materialism (that of Feuerbach included) is that the thing, reality, sensuousness, is conceived in the form of contemplation, but not as sensuous human activity, practice, not subjectively[1].

In this chapter and the next, I try to grasp a specific historical object, late Victorian/early modern novel publishing, as concrete human activity, attempting to describe it as a process which can be known only as a decentered, structured totality, as determinate material practice. Early modern novel production takes its place within a specific social formation, subject to determinations which characterize that larger social formation. But it is also to be understood as relatively autonomous, with its own overdetermined conflicts which make it understandable as a

3

specific practice.[2] Pierre Bourdieu, who chose that quotation from
Marx's "Theses" as the epigraph for *Outline of a Theory of Practice*, suggests three theoretical modes as "moments in a dialectical advance
towards adequate knowledge." Bourdieu recognizes, first, "the truth of
primary experience of the social world," *phenomenological* knowledge,
as in memoirs and autobiographies, from which he distinguishes,
second, the *objectivist* mode, that which "constructs the objective relations (e.g., economic or linguistic) which structure practice and rep-
resentations of practice"; these might be bourgeois political economy
or the narrative social histories or publishing histories I have mentioned. His third mode of theoretical knowledge entails a break (he
counts it as a *second* break) in order to "grasp the limits of objectivist
knowledge,"

> to make possible a science of the *dialectical* relations between the
> objective structures to which the objectivist mode of knowledge
> gives access and the structured dispositions within those structures
> are actualized and which tend to reproduce them.[3]

While making use of the empirical, phenomenological accounts, and
the objectivist attempts to generalize from them, I mean to educe just
such a dialectical knowledge.

I am reading historically a sector of the late Victorian social formation, a society in transition from a high-capitalist, free enterprise mode
of production to the late-capitalist, monopoly-capital mode of production, as Samuel Smiles, so to speak, gives way to Frederick Taylor. The
late Victorian social formation was determined on different levels by
technological change and the flight of capital, by the random mod-
ernization of fixed capital, by imperial markets and increasing international competition, by class struggle and by the growing struggle for
female emancipation. On the economic level, the sector of book production (as indeed some of its products explain ideologically) was
overdetermined by the interplay of these forces, but with a different
temporality. The coming of the Net Book Agreement and the death
of the three-volume novel in the nineties signal that book production
was finally coming to be structured as a patriarchal/capitalist mode of
production.[4] I shall argue that the structural tension between its
"list" and "entrepreneurial" practices marks the contradiction between
the new literary mode of production and the residual petty-commodity

literary mode of production. From the eighties on, ideologies of literary value like those I consider in Chapter 2 structure the ideological level of novel production: ideologies of priority and rarity and of "bestness," patriarchal and international ideologies, overdetermined, again, by the publishing practices I have mentioned. In the last two chapters I examine novels and critical writings as specific instances of these complicated overdeterminations, which are complicated further by the ways in which the literary discourses echo (or overdetermine) each other.

I am attempting to avoid what seems to me the major fault in Peter Keating's *The Haunted Study: A Social History of the Novel, 1875–1914* (1989). To my mind, that very useful study is seriously marred by Keating's contenting himself, as it were, with objectivist knowledge. His method, alternating description with interpretation so as to produce "either a continuous narrative or a series of interrelated narratives," asks these categories ("description," "interpretation," and "narrative") to carry too much weight. His "historical explanation," an "accumulation of . . . demonstrated connections,"[5] stops short of demonstration of these as "concrete human activity," as "practice." His account, I believe, needs to "break" from the empirical, "to bring to light the theory of theory and the theory of practice"[6] inscribed in his objectivist narrative of the early modern novel's social history. For example, in describing the opposition of the Society of Authors to the drafts of publishing contracts proposed by the new Publishers' Association in 1898, Keating tells how the drafts were published in the *Author*, the society's journal, whose editor, the novelist Walter Besant, and the society's secretary, G. Herbert Thring, "took them to pieces clause by clause," Besant demonstrating over and over again how the drafts favored publishers above authors. "It was in many respects," says Keating, "the moment of Besant's greatest triumph" as spokesman for the Society of Authors; but only as seen objectively, we might respond. The missing *dialectical* knowledge is indicated by Keating's uncertainty about the outcome of the episode:

> Besant's triumphant dissection of the model contracts must have played a large part in dispelling whatever willingness there was among the publishers to clarify points of difference. His abrasive approach had served the Society well while it was struggling to establish itself and while its target was the individual publisher: subtler

> methods and a determination to negotiate might just have brought
> a more positive response from the newly-formed Publishers' Associa-
> tion which had at least expressed a wish to improve relations. It is
> also possible that the Society lost more at that particular moment
> than the chance of a "two-sided discussion": in reasserting its hostil-
> ity to the publishers it had won a moral victory, but it lacked the
> power to pursue the advantage it had temporarily gained. The pub-
> lishers regarded the Society's great victory as though it had never
> occurred. (63–64)

The cumulative speculativeness here, "must have played," "might just,"
"is also possible," all mark the inadequacy of Keating's objective knowledge, which a symptomatic reading of the structural determinations
of the episode of the draft contracts can supplant. What is missing,
that is, is a recognition of the structure of historical relations in publishing within which this particular confrontation takes place and
which guarantees the real victory to the publishers. I shall return to
this episode later, after my own attempt to describe the structure of
historical relations, and I mention it here to begin to indicate the difference in purpose and methodology between my own work and
Keating's. For one cannot describe novel production adequately in terms
of intuitions about "willingness," "approaches," moral "determination,"
and "wishes." The "break" I wish to enforce takes the form of an insistence on approaching the early modern novel from the point of view
of its material production within capitalist relations of production. We
must make the effort to think about the material "capitalist relations
of production," a *dialectical* theoretical construct, in order to lift the
description out of an *objectivist*, empiricist problematic. Early modern
novel production must be theorized within the "flux and reflux of capital"[7] in England at the turn of the century, must be viewed as but a
special historical instance of what Marx calls "the transformation of
Commodity Capital and Money Capital into Commercial Capital and
Money-dealing Capital."[8]

I want to read an earlier episode to begin to bring out, as practice,
the relations between authors and publishers and between each of these
and the booksellers in early modern England. On 4 October 1890, in
its coverage of the last day of the weeklong Church Congress, the *Times*
reported on an address by the Rev. Canon F. W. Farrar, archdeacon of
Westminster and author of *Eric, or Little by Little*, on the topic "The

Christian Conception of Commerce," in a session entitled "The Ethics of Commerce." Canon Farrar attacked with "habitual floridity"[9] unethical practices in all branches of contemporary life, calling on his hearers, with his "ardent temperament and unselfish idealism,"[10] "to sweep away from the soil of our national life this heap of dead, putrescent leaves." Amidst his general remarks on adulterated food and so on, Farrar gave a more specific example of unethical practice, taking the opportunity to deplore, as the *Times* summary records it,

> the dishonourable customs which, in many cases, tainted what should be, and often was, the eminently respectable trade of the publisher, and speak of the sweating publishers (hear, hear), who, without a blush would toss to the author perhaps a hundredth part of what, by bargains grossly inequitable, they had obtained.[11]

The uproar following upon this address was immediate, heated, and prolonged. Letters appeared daily in the *Times* for two weeks, from publishers, authors, and officers of the Society of Authors. That body had been founded in 1884 and had established itself to the point of producing, from May 1890, its monthly journal, the *Author*, "conducted by" Walter Besant, who was also, in 1890, the vigorous chair of the society's Committee of Management. The *Author* commented on the Farrar incident, as did the *Bookseller* and, of course, the *Publishers' Circular*, which reprinted a partisan selection from the correspondence (which thus "explains itself").[12] The *Saturday Review, Pall Mall Gazette*, and *St. James Gazette* also commented on the affair. The first letter to the *Times*, from a publisher, J. Russell Endean (who later wrote a triumphant letter summarizing the indictment of Farrar), established the issue which would dominate most of the ensuing debate. Quoting Farrar's offending comment on publishers, Endean asked:

> What have his own publishers to say to the charge? And if his charge in relation to them falls to the ground, then the picture he has presented to the nation is a sham, a cynical libel upon his age, and a dishonour to himself. (7 October, 12)[13]

One day later, Canon Farrar wrote defending himself, arguing "misrepresentation," "hasty reading," "imperfect reports" (8 October, 6), but by then Cassell and Company, publishers of Farrar's *Life of Christ*

(1873), "the biggest 'seller' among religious books of its time,"[14] and his *Life and Works of St. Paul* (1879), had also written to the *Times* giving their view of their relations with him:

> more than 20 years ago we projected a work which was to be a "Popular Life of Christ." The whole scheme of that work as well as its general character was conceived in this house. The idea having been put into a concrete form we entered into negotiations with one or two popular writers for the production of the book; but these negotiations falling through, our attention was drawn to Mr., now Archdeacon, Farrar. It is no disparagement to Archdeacon Farrar's present position to say that at that time (1870) he was comparatively unknown, and had certainly not gained any great reputation in literature. We laid before him the proposal that he should write a "Popular Life of Christ" on the lines suggested by ourselves, and offered him for the copyright of this work the sum of £500, with an additional sum of £100 as a contribution towards the expense of a visit to the Holy Land in connexion with the writing of the work. This offer he accepted, and he duly produced the book which has since attained so wide a fame. . . . Archdeacon Farrar duly received in 1873 the sum we had agreed to pay him for writing the "Life of Christ"; but in consideration of the success of the work we paid him in 1874 an additional sum of £200, in 1875 a further sum of £350, besides an honorarium of £100 for the preparation of an index; in 1876 £200, in 1877 £250, in 1878 £205, and in 1881 £100. Thus for the work for which we had covenanted to pay only £600, and which was absolutely our own property, we voluntarily paid in addition £1,405, making £2,005 in all. We leave your readers to determine whether such action is to be regarded as dishonourable, or whether those who take it are open to the taunt of being "sweating publishers." (8 October, 6)

As a modern commentator, Simon Nowell-Smith, puts it:

> no publisher today, and perhaps few authors, would be likely to find fault with Cassell's for their treatment of Farrar, a writer on whom at the outset, at their own initiative and risk, they had made a speculation, and whom, when that speculation proved unexpectedly remunerative, they recompensed far beyond any written obligation.[15]

Most of the subsequent letters to the *Times* also granted Cassell's position; "in fact," said the *St. James Gazette*, "all the hitting is on one side."[16] But a "hit" must land, and Besant and the Society of Authors, for example, considered that this was not the case. "The main point in the recent controversy in the *Times*," Besant wrote in the *Author*, "was, of course, ignored from the outset."[17] Besant and many of the society's members disagreed with publishers over the relation between author and publisher and over the nature of "literary property," and these understandings controlled their positions in the dispute. Indeed, the correspondence and commentaries on Canon Farrar's charge against publishers imply many of the main determinations of the practice of book production in the 1890s. Cassell's letter, citing "the heavy expenditure on which we embarked" to publish *The Life of Christ*, put in question not only Farrar's renown in 1873 but who was the progenitor of the work. "W.H.P[utnam]" agreed that "the creation of the property was in a very large measure due to the publishers" (10 October, 10), and T. Ralph Price asked "whether it is the publishers who make the authors or conversely the authors who make the publishers" (13 October, 8). "An Author" saw Farrar as simply "the paid clerk of Messrs Cassell's" (11 October, 7), and Andrew Tuer suggested that Farrar was "a hack— let us say the prince of hacks" (14 October, 9). Besant and S. Squire Sprigge raised the matter of the significance of different publishing arrangements (13 October, 8), Besant having introduced the notion of Canon Farrar's "very valuable property" and the nature of his "transaction" with Cassell (9 October, 8). Tuer, a publisher, responded by questioning Besant's understanding of the publishers' "point of view" in producing a book and the matter of investing in a writer's future books, which was the reason for Cassell's extra payments to Farrar (10 October, 10). (Cassell had revealed that Farrar had bargained with another house before accepting a fee for the subsequent *Life of St. Paul*.) These various "truths of primary experience" are the symptoms of the determinate structure I want to examine.

Limited by their at best objectivist understanding, many of the comments in the dispute rely on simple *tu quoque* (another index of the animus: the *Bookseller* asks why Farrar did not condemn "roguish authors" as well as publishers).[18] And what the *Author* called "the deadly rancour shown towards the Society in most of the letters"[19] only matches what we infer to be the intemperate bitterness in Canon Farrar's earlier correspondence with Cassell, which he would not permit to be published.[20] But the anger is again merely an indication of the structural conflict. The public issues of the conflict were objectively undecidable: the matter was not to be settled either by generalizing or by surveying particular cases. The question of whether the author "makes" the publisher, or vice versa, is similarly undecidable. The differences over the contractual arrangement between author and publisher clearly embody radically opposed understandings of their different functions, as "middlemen," "hacks," or whatever, just as the arguments allude to different ideas of the status of past as well as of future publications. While there may be today, as Simon Nowell-Smith suggests, a consensus around the rights and wrongs of Farrar's case, the conflict in 1890 is best understood as symptomatic of the practical struggle over the transformation of the literary mode of production.

Farrar's application to the publishers of the epithet "sweating" was certainly timely, following as it did by only three months the publication of the report of the House of Lords' Select Committee on Sweated Labour. For while C. J. Longman, at the founding of the Publishers' Association in 1896, might speak of the "cordial relations" existing between authors and their publishers,[21] the *Dial*, two years later, carried a report that "for some months now a three-sided discussion of the most heated and acrimonious sort has been going on in England with regard to the mutual relations of the author, the publisher, and the bookseller."[22] The acrimony had been public since the conference held by the Society of Authors in March 1887, on "The Grievances between Authors and Publishers," where Walter Besant had asserted that "the relations between author and publisher are at the present moment most unsatisfactory."[23] Often the publishers' anger was directed at Besant himself. A cartoon in *Punch* in 1891, entitled "Literary Stars," shows among other "Stars" Besant impaling a "sweater" on his quill as he brushes (or kicks) aside John Murray.[24] After "the literary agent," Besant was singled out most often as the cause of the bad feeling between authors and publishers, most unjustly, as S. Squire Sprigge explained:

> He was generally accused of a sweeping hatred of publishers. . . . His real attitude was this: having asserted that ordinary business routine, either carried out personally or by an accredited agent, cannot possibly be opposed to the production of matter of the finest artistic excellence, he set to work to make clear the principles which should

underlie the commercial relations of the author and the publisher. The literary merits of a particular author, the crystal probity of a particular publisher, had nothing to do with the case.[25]

Besant's conduct of the *Author* from 1890 until his death in 1901 was no doubt an affront to publishers, but neither his own merits nor the "crystal probity" of publishers had anything to do with the case. What his detractors were trying to explain (and he, as well, in speaking of "sweating" publishers) were the new structural relations of book production, and the tensions and contradictions that resulted.

An important characteristic of that structure, of earlier origin than and contributing to the animosities, was the differentiation of publishers from booksellers, occasionally acknowledged in memoirs and autobiographies. Samuel Smiles, in his uncomplicated way, was to claim that John Murray II had been "perhaps the first member of the Stationers' craft to separate the business of bookselling from that of publishing."[26] Basil Blackwell was to speak, in the first J. M. Dent Memorial Lecture in 1932, of "the divorce of publishing from bookselling which began with us in the time of Pope," considering the separation "judicious" since "the views of the publisher and the bookseller are different":

> On the broadest lines the publisher takes a relatively small number of big risks, and the bookseller a large number of small risks. Publishers are not concerned with each other's risks; booksellers are concerned with the risks of all publishers indifferently.[27]

While the fact of the differentiation was acknowledged—Robert Buchanan growled, "the Publisher is, at best, only a differentiated, and badly differentiated, Bookseller"[28]—it of course could not at the time be seen other than in an objectivist mode, not, that is, as systemic or structural, as related to other phenomena in the social production of books. Yet if we interrogate this differentiation as an early moment in the process of restructuring book production in late Victorian England, we can see how (as an instance of "structural causality")[29] it caused authors to form their own society, and to respond in other ways as they saw their old relationship to printers and booksellers disappear. Putnam's manual for authors and publishers needed to be revised in 1897 to take account of changes in the practice of producing books:

> In reshaping the material for this revised edition, attention has been
> given to certain phases of literary and publishing methods which
> have come into existence . . . such as the development of authors'
> societies, and the use of literary agencies and "syndicates."[30]

The differentiation of publishers from booksellers, that is to say,
demanded/evidenced a new definition of *publishing* as a specific practice, in its relation to printing and bookselling and authors. And I mean
eventually to point a further differentiation between "list" and "entrepreneurial" publishers.

Publishing as a business, it was said, was poised equivocally between
trade and profession:

> "What exactly do you do?" asks the outsider. "You dont write the
> books, you dont print them and you dont sell them." We publish
> them, is in a word the answer.[31]

But that answer was small comfort to "the thoughtless minds of the
uninitiated, or the suspicious minds of those who have been told that
there is no end of mystery and swindling in the publishing trade."[32]
Publishers themselves defined their position and function in a variety of ways. C. J. Longman suggested that the publisher/author relationship was analogous to that of a solicitor and his client, a formula
which was criticized by Besant in the *Author* for ignoring the real power
struggle.[33] Much of the publishers' mythology derived from a romantic memory of the lives of the publisher booksellers of the era of petty-
commodity book production, of William Blackwood, William and Thomas Longman III, and successive John Murrays. The brothers Longman
"enjoyed (even cosseted) their authors," for instance.[34] Samuel Smiles,
as always, was the perfect purveyor of that image, the drawing room
of John Murray presenting, for example, "the remarkable spectacle of
a single publisher acting as the centre of attraction to a host of distinguished writers." Smiles invited admiration of Murray for "the gran-
deur—for that seems the appropriate word—of his dealings with men
of high genius," as embodied in the episode of Murray freely returning
his quarter share in the ownership of the copyright of *Marmion* to
Scott.[35] While a publisher might indeed be said simply to be someone
who "announces, proclaims or advertises something; one who makes
a thing widely known,"[36] the publishers' idea of the publisher was

often more flatteringly originary: "no matter who might be consulted, Sir Algernon [Methuen] was always the ruling spirit and the constructive force."[37] And after World War I, Basil Blackwell was to proclaim: "the publisher . . . is the captain of industry in the Book World. Directly or indirectly, he employs a small army in the production and distribution of his books."[38] This latter metaphor gestures toward the structural realities of book production which had emerged at the turn of the century, for "broadly speaking, the period as a whole was one in which management was at last beginning to get a solid grip on British industry."[39] Whatever the description or explanation, the tendency of the publisher in the new capitalist book production was to control the entire production of books. The correspondence over Farrar as well as the quarrels over the precise relationship between the publishers and the Society of Authors implies this function of control, although the new relation is masked by the charge that the society (read Walter Besant) "has utterly destroyed the old friendship between authors and publishers which was so pleasant in the days of the first and second Murray."[40]

The publisher's view of the relationship was, of course, far removed from that held by the Society of Authors (and, indeed, from that held by publishers on less ceremonial occasions). Lord Lytton (the second earl of Lytton, and the poet "Owen Meredith") presided at the Society of Authors' conference on "Grievances" in 1887, and presented from the chair a very simple view of the relationship: "in literature, as in other affairs, the public employs two classes of persons—those who produce, and those who distribute," and went on to develop this analysis in a charmingly unsophisticated fashion.[41] Besant, at the same conference, maintained the same distinction but ignored "the public"; "The publishers are the administrators of the great literary property created by the authors." Authors created, publishers simply acted as "administrators, or distributors and collectors, as agents, in short," the relationship Besant would always insist on in his polemics against publishers.[42] In his *Autobiography*, published after his death, he would still express his anger at the publishers who dared appropriate a "literary property" and treat it "as a sacred ark which none but the priests— i.e., those who had it already in their hands—might touch."[43] "Why is a publisher paid at all?" he asked in a letter to the *Athenaeum* on 14 January 1893. "The answer is, 'For his services.' If he administers a property he is paid for his services. For nothing more."[44] He compared the relation to that of two men in the City who agreed to share the profits of an enterprise, and he asked "what would be said in the City . . . *should the one who did the active part refuse to let his accounts be examined?*"[45] It should be noted here that the "partners" concerned themselves with a "property," a text already in some way produced, and, as John Goode says, "the manuscript is thus given a magical ability to operate in the phase of circulation before it becomes a commodity":

> literature is seen [by Besant and the Society] not as a function of the productive process but as a property, protected by law, which in effect acts as a barrier to capitalist investment by demanding a kind of rent—in Marx's terms, a monopoly rent, subject to the laws of demand.[46]

In *The Literary Handmaid of the Church*, the pamphlet from which Farrar took his "sweating" image, Besant repeated that the publisher is simply "an agent . . . managing, distributing, and collecting" around "a very real property"; the publisher is "a man who publishes, undertakes to sell, distribute, and collect money."[47] And in their more heated moments, the society's partisans reduced the publishers further, simply to "tradesmen," the counterpart to the publishers' calling Dean Farrar a "prince of hacks."

The majority of publishers, while paying homage, as we have seen, to their grand predecessors, saw their position in book production very differently from the authors. When they acknowledged, in 1898, "the desirability of consulting the authors before drawing up permanent arrangements for the conduct of a trade in which they are to some extent interested,"[48] they were indicating as well their position of dominance, as capital, in the relations of production. The publisher T. Werner Laurie was so enraged by the iniquity of the Society of Authors and by authors' agents that he felt obliged to warn authors of publishers' real power as capital:

> There is no body of men who could combine as easily as publishers. . . . Fortunately for the Society of Authors and their *clientèle*, they are conservative and reticent beings, but much goading may make them turn, and when they do combine, it is not impossible that they will be in a position to dictate exactly what terms they please both to authors and booksellers.[49]

And William Heinemann (who was, if anyone, Besant's opposite number among the publishers) precipitated an extended correspondence
during the winter of 1892–93 in the *Athenaeum*, *Publishers' Circular*,
and other journals on "the curious condition of the English publisher
of to-day . . . oscillating between the Scylla of those who provide us
with raw material, and the Charybdis of those for whom our ready-made
wares are intended." Heinemann wrote to the *Bookman*: "Let no one
believe the contention that a publisher is merely an agent for placing
a book on the market." Dismissing Besant's apology that an author does
not usually possess a "business mind," Heinemann wrote: "Authors are
misled who rely upon the calculations in the 'Cost of Production' [a
society pamphlet] without that necessary business mind,"[50] and the
publishers and their allies often invoked that particular version of an
objectivist mentality as they enforced their own understanding of the
real relations of book production. In 1945, George Bernard Shaw, who
had been an active member of the Society of Authors at the turn of
the century, was to concur that Besant did not understand publishing
"as a business,"[51] by which he meant, like Heinemann in 1893, that
Besant and the society did not subscribe to the publishers' position,
their particular objectivist reading of the process of book production.

    For authors and publishers were deeply divided over whether "prop-
erty" or "process" was the dominant feature of literary production. The
publishers obviously tended to recognize book production as an
extended process over which they alone should have control. This is
indicated historically by the way that payment by royalty came to supplant the earlier forms of payment of writers: purchase outright of copyright, payment by commission, and payment by "half-profits." A writer
in 1880 described the royalty system in a revealing way. Having presented the pitfalls of the other systems (in which the publisher might
truly be said to be the author's "agent"), he writes:

> You are an author and you offer your work to the "enterprising pub-
> lisher," as it is the fashion to call him. He is to go to the expense of
> paper, printing, binding, advertising, &c., on his *own* account. He is
> then to allow you a certain sum on every copy sold. . . . You would
> thus have no risk.[52]

This writer's emphasis indicates his understanding of the changed
relations of production institutionalized by the royalty system (which

Besant preferred); the author has no risk because he or she has submitted to the publisher's control, *on his own account*, of the production process, often extended into the very gestation of the text, as
was done (albeit within a commission form of contract) with Farrar's
Life of Christ. Thus "phenomenological" accounts of the relations between publisher and author gesture toward divergent objective understandings of the production process around which publishing was
constructed.

The preoccupation of the Society of Authors under Besant with
a preexisting literary property which was simply to be brought to market ultimately derives from an archaic petty-commodity ideology of
production, occasionally shared by some of the older publishers. Longman's statement in his speech to the Publishers' Association in 1896
does not substantially differ, in emphasizing property over production:

> In the first stage of the business between the author and the pub-
> lisher there is an obvious diversity of interest—the diversity which
> always exists between the buyer and the seller. When this stage is
> got over the antagonism should cease, and for the future the inter-
> ests of the two parties should be identical.[53]

Legalistic debates over copyright encouraged this sort of focus on the
exchange value of an object,[54] as did similarly legalistic quarrels over
whether registry at the Stationer's Office or delivery of a copy to the
British Museum actually constituted "publication."[55] In contrast to
these explanations, Heinemann's remark about "raw materials" (*not*
"literary property") implies an objectivist idea of a total process of book
production, controlled by the publisher. As Charles Morgan was to write
in 1943: "The whole movement of books from the author's pen to the
reader's lap is continuous; no part of it is separable from another part;
and this is too little acknowledged—too little sometimes by authors
themselves."[56] But a more radically contrasting, dialectical view of
early modern book production would escape both the phenomenological view of it as the administration and selling of property and the
objectivist, simple capitalist view of it as the manufacture of "raw material" into finished product. For modern publishing is a *structure*, determined not only by the practice of the publisher and the author, but
by the practices of publishers' readers and authors' agents. Moreover
it is a *gendered* structure, and one which produces as a commodity either

an addition to a publisher's "list" or a book to be "boomed" as a "best-seller." "Publishing" is best seen neither as a uniform whole nor as kinds of individual publishers or individual authors or books, but as a distinctive, determinate set of interlocking, often contradictory practices.

Thus we can see that when the *Bookseller*, speaking for publishers at large, considered it ("of course") manifest that, "at least under exist-ing conditions, the interests of the publishers are ultimately insepara-ble from those of the authors on the one hand, and the booksellers on the other,"[57] while it spoke to the old myth of personal friendships, it might well have raised in the nineties the paranoiac fears of both the Society of Authors and the Booksellers' Association insofar as it implied publishers' control of the entire process of book production and dis-tribution. The *Author* spoke in December 1897 of "the Publishing 'Trust'" and noted with alarm two years later that "it is said that we are threatened with a Ring."[58] The publishers, for their part, cited the danger of anarchy, protesting their innocent intent, their desire only to work through standard procedures which also benefited authors and booksellers:

> In their zeal to show that the publisher is not to be trusted, the Committee [of the Society of Authors] have lost sight of the ques-tion at issue. The question is not *how* some form of "control" is to be carried out, but whether there is to be "control" *at all*.[59]

But the Authors' Society believed that the issue (the immediate refer-ence is to the Net Book Agreement) "was not whether there should be control of prices, but how control would work," and their report bris-tled with distrust of publishers and fear of coercion.[60] The coercion or control (here they are speaking of coercion of booksellers) which evoked such distrust was not the personal intervention of a Blackwood, Mur-ray, or Methuen, but rather the intervention and control by structures and specific practices. Shaw said the "Grand Old Men" of the publish-ing world of the nineties "were so powerful that they held the book-sellers in abject subjection," and the booksellers' concern about publishers' plans for the future of their trade is a persistent theme in the *Bookseller* at the end of the nineteenth century.[61] The Society of Authors shared these fears, but was caught in its preoccupation with particular details of the emerging practices.

I have been referring in a general way to "old-line" publishers as being distinct in their practice from certain others, and I want now to make that distinction more precise. It was one which was recognized in various ways at the time. The novelist Hall Caine, for example, addressing a meeting of booksellers at Stationers' Hall on 30 June 1895 on "the present unfair conditions existing in the bookselling trade," referred to the "new" publishers,

> men who rented two rooms somewhere, and without machinery of any visible kind, and almost without visible capital, carried on noisy and apparently profitable businesses by the sole help of the great and powerful distributing agencies.[62]

We may see in this tendentious description, made before an enthusiastically partisan audience, at least the general lineaments of the distinction which is made in other language again and again in the period. One contemporary handbook for authors described the different functions of the "editorial" publisher—"his guiding principle is to publish a book that will 'live,' and the stock and plant of which will not deteriorate"—and the "speculative" publisher, "often a mere gambler in the copyrights of 'star' authors," who is interested in immediate success, "getting a quick return for the capital invested in the purchase of copyright and cost of production."[63] In his extension of Mumby's history of publishing, Ian Norrie recognizes in the nineties "established publishers" (in a chapter with a "dynastic ring") and the "new imprints," but he does not explain the distinction as other than simply chronological.[64] And yet, although members of the Society of Authors might accuse publishers generally of "over-enterprise," and while these functions might combine in a single house, they came to represent, as Leopold Wagner put it, "marked types."[65] A recent study of the sociology of publishing talks of the ways of distinguishing what it calls "publishing worlds" or "sectors within the industry" (and what I would call "publishing ideologies"): large and small firms, "core" and "peripheral" firms, and "consumer-" and "producer-oriented" firms. Their reference to Pierre Bourdieu's distinction between "short term" and "long term" publishing decisions,[66] relating to the turnover time of publishing capital, more nearly captures the emphasis I am trying to make. For these types are symptoms of countervailing historical tendencies within contemporary capitalist publishing ("the transformation of Commodity Capital into Commercial Capital and Money-dealing Capital"), which I shall settle on calling *"list"* and *"enterprising"* (or *"entrepreneurial"*).

The changed function of the "publisher's reader" is another symptom of the new relations of book production at the turn of the century. Even in their earlier incarnation as "booksellers," publishers had of course had literary advisors, "usually an author of high standing, whose word is accepted as final by the publisher." [67] As Arthur Waugh was to write: "the literary adviser of the mid-Victorian era was ... a sort of mysterious soothsayer, imprisoned in some secret back room, and referred to cryptically as 'our reader.' " [68] John Blackwood had Colonel Blackwood and others, and when George Meredith began his association with Chapman and Hall in 1860 he was succeeding John Forster. But in the relations between writer and publisher emerging at the turn of the century the reader's position and function changed. B. W. Matz, of Chapman and Hall, wrote that "Mr Meredith's word was the final one with us in almost every circumstance," like that of other "early" readers, such as Forster, John Morley, Andrew Lang, "Q," and Edward Garnett:

> Most of them, before becoming literary advisors, had established themselves as novelists or poets; ... and in general, they had a rather thorough knowledge of the profession or trade of publishing before becoming readers. [69]

Arthur Waugh, in 1930, recognized two distinct standards upon which a publisher's reader may set to work:

> A reader may say to himself: "I have the credit of the house in my hands, and it is not to be given over to the Philistines. Our programme is to publish sound literature, so far as we can, and to decline to lower the public taste...." Or, on the other hand, he may say: "I am paid by my employers to find them books that will be profitable investments. The public taste is low, but that is nothing to do with me." [70]

Meredith and these others were of the first type and were associated with the old-line, "list" publishing houses and a generally petty-commodity ideology. Linda Marie Fritschner has recently shown how these two ideologies were overdetermined by readers' practices. The one type, which she represents by Edward Garnett (Jonathan Cape) "discovered, encouraged and worked directly with authors":

> He revised manuscripts but often the kinds of advising he did went below the surface to touch upon the theme, motivation and structure of a novel.

Fritschner represents the other type of reader by Geraldine Jewsbury, reader for Bentley's, who "rarely had contact with authors":

> Her services were primarily on behalf of the publisher, only secondarily on behalf of the authors, and least of all on behalf of literature. She tried to uphold literary standards within the category of literature as an entertainment or a diversion. Generally her acceptance or rejection of a manuscript depended upon her evaluation of the commercial potential of the manuscript.

I think that Fritschner's general conclusion is important in placing the publisher's reader in the structured practice of early modern publishing: "Although the patterns of relationships among readers, authors, and publishers differed, the readers, because they advised on the acceptance, rejection, and revision of manuscripts . . . had substantial power in shaping policy within a publishing firm."[71] But also her distinction between the two types of publishers' readers is important; the contrast in readers' practice which she finds between Garnett and Jewsbury indicates the larger transformation we are locating, as in the course of the century the reader's loyalties shift more decidedly to his or her employer, as "personal" relations give way to commercial, capitalist relations and, most important for our discussion in the next chapter, as the "category of literature" changes. While the capitalist tendency is always toward "profitable investments," some publishers might, like Stanley Unwin in 1926, disparage as "a depressing business" a list consisting of "nothing but Tarzans and Rosaries [turn-of-the-century bestsellers]," and yearn for a more ideal reader:

> To most publishers who are keen on their job, the sound literary judgement of an Arnold Bennett would be the first and chief ingredient in an ideal reader, though they would not underrate both the

necessity and desirability of throwing in a little of Bennett's commercial acumen and *flair*.[72]

In a very similar way, the rise of the "literary agent" is symptomatic of the capitalist transformation of the relations of publishing. The Society of Authors itself had been founded, as Besant so frequently pointed out, to advise authors on the development of their "literary property." Every issue of the *Author* was prefaced by advice on "How to Use the Society" and for several years by a notice for "The Authors' Syndicate," which was created as an autonomous body to "take charge of the business of members of the Society."[73] This historical situation, as Frank Swinnerton says, also produced the agent.[74] In 1893 Besant published a list of reasons why an author might want to employ an agent, that is, "a man of business to make our arrangements for us with a man of business," and in the same issue he warned members to be very careful in dealing with an agent: "Your only safety is in consulting the Society, or some friend who has had personal experience of the agent."[75] Besant dismissed the charge that agents had destroyed the friendly relationship between publisher and author, but one point of his advice acknowledges the evolving structural relations of publishing. He remarked in 1892 that an agent is very useful to the writer who has already created a demand,[76] and again in 1893,

> The young writer who is as yet unknown and has no *clientèle* does not want an agent. Let him work on, making some kind of a name for himself gradually or by a single *coup*. When he has done so an agent may advantageously take him in hand.[77]

Besant is never more precise than this about the agent's function, perhaps because it contradicts his main emphasis on "property" over "process." His statement in 1893 was a response to a sardonic attack on agents, "The Middleman as Viewed by a Publisher," which Heinemann had published in the *Athenaeum* in November. There, having alleged that the typical agent's policies were *suaviter in modo* and self-assertion, Heinemann had turned to the agent's "business," which he saw as looking out for "the author who has hitherto been unsuccessful, who is just beginning to succeed, and who has found a friend in some publisher, whose endeavours and efforts and work have at least helped to bring him into recognition."[78] For Heinemann, "whose enterprise and energy were inexhaustible," the literary agent was a nuisance, doing more harm than good by interfering with an enterprising publisher's attempts to organize production of texts. His biographer claims: "to the less enterprising, less energetic and less competent publisher [literary agents] were a boon," colluding with those "new" publishers who were "continually poaching on his preserves."[79] But it was the very conditions of publishing that gave rise to the "enterprising" publisher which produced the agent as well. And what particularly exercised the publishers and their supporters was precisely the situation which Besant and Heinemann had remarked. T. Werner Laurie, too, attacked the agent as "an unpleasant excrescence on literature" for intervening between an author and a publisher who, having "discovered" and promoted in various ways and lost money on the author's first book, hopes that a new book by the same author "may bring him 'level on the deal'":

> This is the advantageous moment for the agent to step in. He writes to the author, saying he can get him an extra five or seven and a half per cent royalty. He has no more idea than the man in the moon what publisher will give this, but he is aware that he has only to take the manuscript to any young firm which is anxous to have a name that has been well advertised on their list, to get the necessary promise at once. The author in nine cases out of ten bites. The young firm publish the work, but owing to their having insufficient experience and trade connection it fails flat, and the result is a loss to both author and publisher. We have no hesitation in saying that this is a sample of dozens of cases which have occurred during the last two or three years.

Laurie then accuses agents of being responsible for "driving" (or sweating) novelists. Persuaded by an agent, "the author finds himself turned into a fiction mill with contracts staring him in the eyes for three or four novels a year, for the next, say, five years."[80] Again, the angry tone of these accusations is part of their historical meaning, indicating the reality of the conflict among authors, publishers, and booksellers. This was not just a falling out among friends. A less angry, broader, historical understanding would place the new literary agent at the very heart of the new relations of publishing. The new terms of trade were necessarily contradictory, and the agent, like the publisher's reader,

functioned to mediate the contradiction, distributing advantage according to the circumstances of his hiring—I know of no female agents in
the nineties. The offense which the agent gives, personifying the hag-
gling of the marketplace for some authors and "intruding" for some
publishers, arises in each case from the agent's addressing the actual
contemporary process of book production and looking for advantage
there. To a holder of "literary property" there was no process; to an
enterprising publisher the process was his to control, without outside
intervention. The conspicuous, controversial presence of the agent calls
attention to these conflicting views and to the real historical process
which they confusedly address. Literary agents were called into being
by the antagonisms already caused by the changing relations of literary
production, and by the consequent emergence of newly exploitable
literary rights.

The particular set of relations which most pervasively determined
the structure of publishing as it changed were patriarchal relations.
Sylvia Walby's recent book, *Patriarchy at Work*, presents a model of a
complex system of patriarchy, a system of relatively autonomous structures in articulation with capitalist relations, which would allow us to
examine early modern publishing as a gendered totality.[81] Walby
defines patriarchy as a system of interrelated social structures through
which men exploit women, explaining gender relations at the level of
the social system rather than at the objectivist level of discrete social
institutions (as is done, for instance, in Tuchman and Fortin's analysis
of publishers' readers).[82] The value of Walby's analysis lies in its
reference not to individuals or to particular practices but to the ex-
ploitative *structures*, such as "the patriarchal mode of production,"
domestic labor. Within the relations of publishing it does not crucially
matter whether a particular woman writer is married or unmarried,
nor indeed whether we are talking specifically about women writers.
Patriarchal relations determine not only the patriarchal mode of production, but paid work, sexuality, the state, and male violence in the
social formation as a whole, for "the patriarchal mode of production
necessarily exists in articulation with another mode of production."[83]
When the patriarchal mode of production engages with the capitalist
mode of production—as in the patriarchal/capitalist literary mode of
production at the end of the century—the control of women's labor
is of primary importance. Control is achieved both by excluding women

from paid work on the same terms as men and by downgrading the work
they do, as well as, of course, by limiting female management of capital.
Walby lists several forms of patriarchal control or determination, among
which are denial of educational opportunity and restriction on the
amount of certain kinds of work that women may do:

> these exclusionary practices exist in varying forms of directness,
> from rigid rules which are consistently enforced, such as the ban on
> women taking degrees at universities in the UK before the late nine-
> teenth century, to more direct forms which may not always produce
> the same effect, such as the 'last-in, first-out' practice in redundancy
> situations.[84]

It is here that the particulars of the work of Tuchman and Fortin on
the exclusionary practices of publishers' readers are more relevant, as
well as the downgrading (as "silly") of the work of "lady novelists" over
the course of the century, matters to which I shall return in the next
chapter. But the agents of exclusionary practices were also often male-
dominated organizations like the Society of Authors, which excluded
women writers from its Committee of Management in its early years.
A mode of male control more specific to the profession of authorship
was the disparagement which peppers the pages of the *Author*, as in the
article "Women in Journalism" in 1892 which asked the not entirely
unprejudiced question "Is the effect produced on journalism by this
invasion of women a salutary one?"[85] This writer also exemplifies the
recurring references in the *Author* to the use of "feminine wiles" by aspir-
ing female writers, instances of "forms of sexuality which are perceived
as appropriate to their gender roles":

> The problem has puzzled a good many of us, as to the reason that
> certain ladies, whose scholarship is as little evident as their shyness,
> are in the happy position of realizing large incomes. A reason given
> me by an artless and pretty young journalist, might be of some use
> to the future novelist [a "female Thackeray," writing "the real genuine
> life of the woman journalist"]: "Oh, it's quite easy to get work if the
> Editor's 'gone on you.'"[86]

In the same tone of violation, another issue of the *Author* commented
on "The Literary Ladies' Dinner": "A dinner where the guests are all
ladies seems to the undisciplined mind an insipid thing; but then

undisciplined minds are not invited."[87] I shall return to the determinations of patriarchy in early modern literary production in my discussion of the patriarchal determinations of ideologies of literary value in the next chapter, but here I mean to emphasize different ways in which patriarchy is determinant on the economic level of publishing.

Finally, I want to expand somewhat my point that these changing relations were accompanied by, or produced, a changed understanding of the nature of the text, considered as a commodity. Whereas Walter Besant, as we have seen, naively considered the production process to be one in which an author, no businessman him- or herself, hired various agents to assist in distributing the already produced text, the two ideological practices in publishing, "list" and "enterprising," constructed the text as a source either of steady or of sudden and immense profit, each in a different relation to the publishing process. The concurrence among Besant, Heinemann, and Laurie about the literary agent's point of entry indicates the real economic issue. Another commentator is more explicit: the object of publishers' concern is not the immediate text but, in some form or other, *future* texts: the agent's intervention makes overt the publisher's interest in future texts, as the publisher must either pay more for the future work of an author, "whose name would be a credit to his 'list,'"[88] or do without it, as was suggested in Cassell's account of their relations with Archdeacon Farrar after the success of *The Life of Christ*. At issue is future work, and indeed one way for a publisher to conceive of that issue is to speak of a "list." When G. Herbert Thring, in 1926, wrote his (unpublished) history of the Society of Authors, he noted that "some forty years ago the future book clause [in book contracts] was practically unknown." Thring ascribed the arrival of the future book clause to the publishers' desire to counter the society's encouraging its members to demand higher royalties by revealing details of publishers' costs and profits. But it also arose in relation to other elements in the emerging structure of publishing, as a response to, or an anticipation of, the activities of agents, for instance. Some publishers, Thring claimed, went so far as to demand rights of first refusal for an author's next six books, and the *Author* regularly denounced in its pages "the old trick" of persuading authors into "binding themselves down for future books with the same publisher."[89] The matter of future rights was obviously central to the publishers' concerns at this moment in publishing history. While Dickens in his time, like other popular authors, was plagued by future commitments he had made, my point is that here the notion of future rights is being integrated into the "standard" contractual relation between all writers and their publishers. During the squabble over Farrar's *Life of Christ*, Andrew Tuer, publisher, corrected Walter Besant who had implied Farrar's right to the extra payments he received; Tuer wrote: "The extra payments made to the author of a successful book are not made as a matter of right, but with the purely selfish object of again securing his services."[90] The *Author*, of course, saw the issue in its usual way, as infringing on the personal rights of an independent author seeking to market his or her "literary property," and in 1899 Besant criticized a draft contract which had been shown to the society on precisely those terms:

> To bind oneself to a publisher for another book is at all times a very dangerous matter. If the publisher treats an author fairly in the first instance he would know that the author would return to him with his second book.[91]

The preoccupation with "futures" indicates more than the interest in developing authors shown by "list" publishers. Meredith, for example, as a reader for Chapman and Hall, had often advised that a "book will not do, . . . but the author strongly encouraged," or "By all means encourage the lady."[92] Here his language of "encouragement" indicates the personal as well as the "enterprising" nature of his advice. But Geraldine Jewsbury, as we have seen, attempted as a reader to focus more specifically on the commercial potential of the particular manuscript, the purpose being a more immediate success rather than the long-term benefit in adding the book to Bentley's list. Meredith and Jewsbury were each no doubt simply following their firm's policy, and the point here is that these individual policies were being subsumed in a "standard" policy for the industry as a whole.

These changing structural relations of publishing again show themselves in the quarrel over what Besant called "the name of the publisher." Besant made inquiries to see whether other authors shared his opinion that the reading public did not care about the name of the publisher of a book:

> The reply from the general reader has been mostly to the effect that he cares no more about the name of the publisher than the name of

the printer. Two or three reply that they know Dent's books to be wonderfully got up, and that they like John Lane's books for the same reason.

One of his correspondents confessed that "I have never troubled myself with the name of the publisher":

> I know the names of Longman and Murray, and one or two more, I suppose, but I do not think they have any more to do with the contents of the book than the paper-maker.[93]

Here one can begin to sympathize with the older publishers' irritation at the authors' arrogance; Besant is blinded (and presumably he blinds his informants by the form of his question) by his preoccupation with the publishing firm as a distinct, momentary phenomenon, as a "name" in the simplest sense. What these publishers, on the other hand, are preoccupied with, what they would see as signified by "name," is, as we have seen, what they called a "list." "[Authors] have not grasped," wrote Frank Swinnerton in the 1930s, ". . . the fact that the publisher lives by his list, and not by the individual books in it."[94] Another writer concurs: "It does not seem to be recognized that book publishers have lists which reflect a certain trend or trends of thought and practice."[95] There were various ways a publisher might personalize its list, for example, by its books' "design," or more broadly, by its "house style," so that its books were "recognizable as members of one family":

> a good individual style, consistently followed in all a publisher's books, . . . inseparable from the firm itself, developing into a tradition for it, growing and changing gradually as is the way with all good tradition.[96]

Clearly the "name" which these "list" publishers were concerned with was more than the name as Besant understood it. No longer grounded on the personality of a John Murray, it signified a corporate, capitalist identity, a "textual" identity distinct as a commodity from the text which a Besant imagined; the text which these firms sold was sold, as Frederick Macmillan put it, "to the public which buys books published by our firm."[97] The "list," for such a publisher, was thus distinct from that of earlier, petty-commodity book producers, who did not so clearly see it as developing into a "tradition" for the firm, which was then marketable as the primary commodity:

> by "list" a publisher designates those books five, ten, twenty years old which sell without advertising their fifty, two hundred or a thousand copies every year, that are his "bread and butter," and which pay his overhead expenses.[98]

But it was distinct also from the commodity marketed by the "new," "enterprising" publisher. For whereas the "list" text realizes its surplus value over time, the "enterprising" text realizes its surplus value immediately, and often finally.

It's at this point that I can begin to theorize publishing as a decentered totality in transition. For the history of publishing in the nineteenth century is not properly the history of the "development" of a coherent process, or even of a coherent process "in transition." Seen dialectically, it is rather the history of a process of self-constitution (as capitalist book production, i.e., as "publishing") among authors, booksellers, and *soi-disant* publishers. Unlike the petty-commodity production of three-decker novels in the mid-nineteenth century, which was part of a pre-capitalist structure involving primarily the lending libraries, the process is now one of the capitalist production of commodity texts. But the conflictual relations I have been discussing express "a double situation":

> On the one hand, . . . circulation has still not mastered production, but is related to it simply as its given precondition. On the other hand, . . . the production process has not yet absorbed circulation into it as a mere moment.[99]

The "list" publishers we have been talking about are the inheritors of the Murrays, Longmans, and Blackwoods, and indeed, of the printer-booksellers of the eighteenth century, the bearers of "trading" or "commercial" capital, which is older, as Marx says, than the capitalist mode of production. In this "list" sector (or ideology) of publishing capital, "the product becomes a commodity through trade." The "list" (or "name") which is so important to these publishers simply signifies that form of the process of turning a book into a commodity: "It is trade that shapes the products into commodities; not the produced commodities whose movement constitutes trade." But in *fully capitalist production*, Marx argues, the production and circulation processes become one: "the production process is completely based on circulation, and circulation is a mere moment and a transition phase of production." Thus, whereas "list" publishing is simply money capital exclusively designed for buying and selling, and never assumes the form of productive capital but remains "list," forever "penned into capital's circulation sphere," "enterprising" publishing of best-sellers is fully capitalist production, where the merchant takes direct control of the whole production process and "the merchant becomes an industrialist directly." [100]

When they are rethought in these terms, the empirical details I have been recounting can be seen as the traces of a decentered structure, the indignation and bitterness, I have suggested, arising from the uncomprehending, contradictory (phenomenological) positions within the structure. I have spoken of the " 'list' sector or tendency," and by this I mean to indicate that there is no necessary correlation between the empirical historical categories of publisher, "established/new," and the theoretical historical categories, "list"/"enterprising" (into which I have translated "commercial capitalist" and "fully capitalist"). While in the 1870s and 1880s that correlation seemed usual (i.e., there appeared to be "sectors"), "list" and "enterprising" represent historically different tendencies toward capitalist accumulation in publishing, and during this particular period of historical transformation they are in a contradictory relation, which underlies not only the confusions of a Walter Besant but antagonisms between publishers and authors which will be resolved (temporarily) only by the institution of "modern publishing methods." And so, while Besant saw Archdeacon Farrar (and Farrar had come to see himself) from within a petty-commodity ideology as the producer of a "literary property," a pre-, or noncapitalist way of understanding, Cassell, an "enterprising" publisher, saw Farrar as simply labor power, a means of production in a process which they controlled of producing a "popular" text, that is, not one to be valued as part of one's list (the silence during the correspondence of such "list" publishers as the Murrays and Longmans is no accident). And the issue of whether the author "makes" the publisher, whether Farrar was making Cassell, or vice versa, is thus settled by the enterprising capitalist mode of production into which Farrar, whatever he and Besant thought, had entered. Had John Murray, on the other hand, accepted for inclusion in their list another sort of "Life of Christ," Farrar might be said to some extent to have helped "make" John Murray. The two kinds of publisher's reader, of course, indicate either the "enterprising" or "list" bias of a publisher, and the literary agent, as I have suggested, is called forth precisely to enable the new entrepreneurial publishers to locate appropriate authors, and authors generally to cope with enterprising publishers. As well, the two capitalist publishing practices, the one (list) embodying commercial capital and the other (enterprising) productive capital, imply two different conceptions of commodity text (as contrasted to the commodity book of mid-nineteenth-century petty-commodity production): a conception of text determined (often by "design" and "house style") by a "list," and a conception of "text" in which under control of the publisher a popular best-seller is produced, which passes as commodity capital through the circulation sphere and is finally sold as a use-value. I want to conclude by commenting briefly on the episode of the publishing agreements which Peter Keating assessed objectively in *The Haunted Study*.

While they disliked the stridency of Walter Besant's objections to the draft agreements in 1896, the editors of the *Academy* felt that "the Authors' Society comes off best," and the *Athenaeum* too ("a journal not suspected . . . of undue partiality to authors")[101] thought the Publishers' Association had made a mistake in making the proposals public: "one would almost think that they were a caricature by an embittered author of the demands of the typical publisher."[102] Kipling agreed, in the pages of the *Author*, as did all those who wrote to the society in the next three months, with "complete unanimity of condemnation."[103] Besant had published in the *Author* from time to time his position on agreements:

> it is not generally understood that the author, as the vendor, has the absolute right of drafting the agreement upon whatever terms the transaction is to be carried out. In every other form of business, the right of drawing the agreement rests with him who sells, leases, or has control of the property.[104]

The society's active membership concurred. Thring, as its secretary, sent to the members copies of the proposed agreements along with his own critique and that of Besant, and his covering letter spoke of how such contracts would "impoverish" the position of literature, how an author would be "irretrievably degraded into . . . dependence upon the casual generosity of a tradesman." [105] Besant imagined, from his some-what confused position on the rock of "literary property," that the present situation, produced by the publishers' proposed agreements, represented "a revolution in the prospects and position of literature." "It is said," he warned, "that we are now threatened with a Ring. . . . All the conditions necessary for a Ring have been attempted and are being attempted. Against these attempts we have the Society of Authors—that are nothing else—to protect us." [106] When the Publish-ers' Association offered to confer about the draft agreements, the Com-mittee of the Authors' Society, sure of its moral position and its power, "refused to hold any conference on these documents." [107]

What had failed Besant and the society were their analyses both of the agreements and of "the present situation," the politics of the "deadlock," as John Murray labeled it in a speech to the Third Inter-national Congress of Publishers in June 1899. For the British publish-ers were not acting in isolation. The Second International Congress, meeting in Brussels in 1897, had heard a paper recommending "a code of usages concerning the relations between authors and publishers," and had set up a "Mixed Commission" on the matter which presented to the 1899 congress a "Memorandum of the Rules in Use and Points to be foreseen in the Relations between Authors and Publishers." [108] Besant himself foresaw very little; his own critique of the agreements again simply rang the changes on his pet topics: literary property and the independence of the author, the insignificance of a publisher's "name," and the absence of "risk" in publishing. Thring's critique was a more sophisticated version of Besant's. But while Thring too attacked the agreements' vagueness about accounting procedures and worried about details of wording and publishers' good faith, some of his other concerns indicate how the publishers were more completely in con-trol of the revolution in the prospects of literature than the Society of Authors understood. Thring was puzzled that the publishers had not put forward any draft agreement for the outright purchase of copyright, not recognizing that such petty-commodity, "literary property" rela-tions were no longer appropriate in the new edifice the publishers were constructing. Similarly futile, because similarly out of date, was his ob-jection to the publishers' empowering their "executors, administrators, and assigns." "The contract," Thring wrote, "is between principal and agent, and is a personal contract." Yet the *Publishers' Circular,* throughout the nineties, announced the incorporation of publisher after publisher as a limited company, necessitating more corporate forms of negotiation and contract. Again, while the danger in the publishers' arrogation of exclusive rights to produce and publish works in the English language throughout the world is easier for Thring to recognize, he overlooks the crucial next clause: "The Publisher shall have the entire control of the publication and sale and terms of the book." Besant noticed this: "the publishers propose to put the clock back and now lay claim to the whole of literary property—its entire management and nearly all the emoluments." But again he saw it as control of "property" rather than of process, as his sense of what the clock was recording would indicate. And again, while Thring was moved to object to the publishers' invocation of "customary trade terms" as arbitrary, he too responded as if the question were simply one of the prices asked for a literary property, rather than management or control of the production process. As John Murray noted in a speech to the annual meeting of the Publishers' Association in 1899, none of the commentaries by the Society of Authors recognized the publishers' distinction between "the bargains which must go before" and the agreements themselves, "which are a very different thing."[109] The society's preoccupation with literary property had again blinded them to the ways in which the production of books was being restructured by capitalist publishers, with the agreements assuming but distinguishing the prior bargaining from decisions in the production process itself, over which they sought sole control.[110]

It is Thring's and Besant's blindness and oversights, determined by their petty-commodity ideology of literary property, in the face of the publishers' bold attempt finally to structure publishing as the capitalist production of texts worldwide, rather than Besant's abrasiveness or refusal to negotiate, which indicate the historical significance of the episode of the draft contracts. Three years later the *Author* was to apply a sarcastic label, "Mr. Absolute," to a publisher whose agreement they analyzed, and again their position was beside the historical point. That agreement tried to assign to a publisher

> in his absolute discretion . . . the right to sell, exchange, assign, or otherwise dispose of all and every right of publication or of translation . . . on any terms and for any period and either wholly or partially or exclusively or otherwise as he shall think expedient. . . .[111]

Thring's gloss traces the extremes of "Mr. Absolute's" claims but is unable to comment on the position from which such power might be claimed. The confidence signified by what Thring labels "absolutism" represents a moment in the final transformation of publishing into a capitalist structure. The publishers had begun openly to recognize that whatever the Society of Authors might say, the new practice of publishing ensured their complete control of the process. Ironically, in the same issue of the *Author* in which the draft agreements were commented on, Besant complained about the current proceedings of the House of Lords Committee on the Law of Copyright. As Besant said, although authors are not necessarily the slaves of publishers, the hearing almost suggested that. "What happened?" he asked:

> The committee meet. The first person they call is a publisher: the second person they call is a publisher: the third person they call is a publisher. Up to the time of writing these remarks no author has been called at all. Perhaps none will ever be called.[112]

Exactly. As Peter Keating says about the affair of the draft agreements, "The publishers regarded the Society's great victory as though it had never occurred." And well they might; the new structure (or "situation") with its two versions of capitalist publishing practice meant that the publishers could ignore the Society of Authors. Walter Besant, "Captain of the Fleet—the bravest of them all," as the *Author* called him, died in June 1901, and G. Herbert Thring succeeded him as editor of the *Author*.[113] Besant's death seems to have ended the attempts by the Society of Authors to intervene in the changes which had overtaken publishing practices. Thring remained as the society's secretary until 1928, and he records in his "History of the Society of Authors" an episode which not only indicates his own frustration but is again symptomatic of the new situation. The struggle between publishers and authors had indeed abated, or its form had changed, by the time Thring retired. In 1928, Lord Gorell (Ronald Gorell Barnes, third Baron Gorell) was elected chair of the society's Committee of Management, "surprisingly," as Victor Bonham-Carter says, because Gorell was allowed to combine that post with his partnership in the firm of John Murray.[114] Thring, who had written a book, *The Marketing of Literary Property*, wrote Gorell asking for the support of the society in making its contents known to the members. In Thring's account of the episode, Gorell replied that "it would be useless to refer the matter to the Committee as he had been requested to dissociate the Society from its Publication." With some bitterness, Thring's memoir attributes to such decisions as this the decline of membership in the Society of Authors in the twenties; "the work of the Committee," he wrote, "which used to take a prominent place in the pages of 'The Author' now fills hardly a page and is hidden among the advertisements at the end as if it was ashamed of itself." [115] But from another point of view, the "shameful" placing of the committee's minutes in the *Author*, the decision not to promote Thring's book on literary property, and the anomalous position of a publisher as chair of the society's Management Committee all simply indicate the new historical situation in publishing. Like all nostalgia, Thring's ignores the forces which produce historical change; while "a formidable champion of authors' rights," Thring was also "inflexible," less politically astute than Walter Besant, and although he continued to analyze in the *Author* the offending clauses in publishers' contracts, he could not see that the society's moment of relative power had clearly ended, that book publishing was now fully constituted as a sector of commercial capital: corporate, enterprising, and modern. As a recent publishing historian has put it, "The distinction between 'good' and 'bad' publishers is no longer felt to apply in these more professional days," [116] and the massive elisions in her phrase "more professional days" definitively mark the historical change.

2. Valorizing "the Literary"

WHILE the ideologies of "enterprise" and "list" determine every capitalist publisher's specific practice of publishing, varying in determinate weight from publisher to publisher and from book to book, it would be a mistake to turn now to an analysis of the publishing practice of one particular publisher, and then another, and another, or to the production history of particular books. A marxist economist might attempt in that way to work out the organic composition of the capital in a publishing house and the relation of that composition to "entrepreneurial" or "list" practices, or even the organic composition of the capital in the production of a specific book, but the larger picture of capitalist publishing as a dialectical process, and of a book as a moment in that process, would be lost, and that larger dialectical process is precisely what I want to explore. Building on the analysis of early modern publishing as capital in the last chapter, I want now to analyze some of the determinate historical practices within and through which the late Victorians constructed ideologies of literary value. I am attempting again to see these practices dialectically; it will be important to insist upon the overdetermination[1] of these materials, in that they not only are determined by capitalist publishing but also in turn determine publishing practices, for "literary value," determined historically by such specific practices as those I shall discuss, took a different emphasis or configuration as *value* depending on whether the publisher's ideology was "enterprising" or "list." The entrepreneurial publisher drew on perceptions of literary value different from those of the publisher of an established list, and these different emphases, as practices, in turn dictated what the writer might produce. Another way of stating my purpose is to say that I am attempting here to analyze what is usually described simply as the late Victorian "market for books," or "late Victorian taste," but trying to avoid the ideologically foreclosing term "market," with its residual connotations of free, honest, individual buyers and sellers meeting in a common, village space, to exchange simple, straightforward commodities. In the third edition of his *Library Manual* (1892), J. H. Slater, a bibliographer, advised sellers and buyers of rare books that "in order to estimate the value of books with any degree of correctness, considerable experience, combined with a thorough knowledge of the market, is required." He asserted two main principles: "First, that popular taste points out what books to buy and what to avoid; and, secondly, that the booksellers regulate their prices according to the demand."[2] But when we consider these principles in relation to the marketing of new books, we encounter the techniques by which "popular taste" may be manipulated entrepreneurially to create a specific demand. Alternatively, we can see that it might be difficult to assign a price to a book which "popular taste" might take some months or years to locate in a publisher's list. Rather than seeing an idealized "market" in actual late Victorian book production and distribution practice, I shall examine it as informed by the interaction of the ideologies of "enterprise" and "list," which I have located in its decentered structure, in their relation to specific *structures of valorization*, distinct discourses of *value: economic* valorization because this is the moment (C–M') in capital's production/exchange process (M–C–M') where the surplus value produced is realized as profit[3]; but also *ideological* valorization because this is the moment in which the imagined use-value of books is constructed and sustained, overdetermining the book's exchange-value. And so in this chapter I present brief analyses of four different ideological moments, four structures of valorization, that is, of the production of "literature" or "the literary" as commodity in late Victorian and early-twentieth-century England.

In general, my procedure will be, again, to read a concrete historical situation or episode symptomatically, drawing on objectivist accounts but pointing up the implied dialectical relations. I intend that these readings interact by implication in a conception of "the literary" for which I shall present no further definition, rather returning in the concluding section of the chapter to "enterprise" and "list." My four particular instances are not meant to be exclusive; the historical process of constructing "literary value" has no limits and my choice of four simply represents my own limitations of time and present capability. The episodes I examine here are (relatively) autonomous, enough so to cause, perhaps, initial consternation: book collecting; the determination of the "best" books; the constitution of a patriarchal/capitalist literary mode of production; and the institution of international copyright. Some of these instances have been studied elsewhere, and I shall want to draw on those discussions, taking advantage of their familiarity but rereading symptomatically the historical debates and conflicts as contributing to the shaping of discourses of literary value, as correcting and supplementing each other (that is, as overdetermined), and then as overdetermining entrepreneurial and list publishing practices.

1. The most obvious instance of early modern entrepreneurial publishing might be said to be the career of the bibliographer-forger Thomas J. Wise. For while years of bibliographical study have been devoted to showing that Wise's forgeries were unique in their day and that Wise had willing accomplices, Harry Buxton Forman or whoever, the histories of the forgeries make it clear that not only their unmasking in the 1920s and early thirties by John Carter and Graham Pollard but also Wise's very practice as a forger was historically determined. It was no accident that a Thomas J. Wise should enterprisingly manipulate the rare book market from the mid-1880s until the 1920s. I take the analyses of Carter and Pollard, and of Michael Sadleir, of bibliographical practice and the first edition market as recording the constitution of certain specific discourses of value in book collecting at the turn of the century, discourses that produced the conditions for Wise's activities by contributing to an ideological construction of "the literary." Earlier bookmen had not been "first edition collectors" in the modern sense. Carter and Pollard trace in the *Enquiry* the slow transformation from collecting "the magnificence of early printing and early illustration, the work of the classic binders, all the physical splendour of books,"[4] to the nineteenth-century mode of book collecting, "the type of collecting which is characteristic of the last fifty years" (i.e., from 1885) (100). The change began in the 1870s, as the distance in time between collectors and the objects of their enthusiasm lessened and as interest in collecting books became more personal and "sentimental" (100–101). What the influential poet-collector Frederick Locker-Lampson brought to book collecting in the 1880s was not simply an interest in "the masterpieces (and the masterpieces only) of English literature from Chaucer to Swinburne," but a preoccupation with their rarity and with what Carter and Pollard call their "historical"

importance, "history" here being the interplay between biography and the circumstances of publication (101). For the decade of the eighties marked a "revolution" in collectors' practice, accompanying the foundation of societies for the study of individual authors and the production of modern author bibliographies.[5] James Nelson describes the conditions surrounding the founding of the Bodley Head in 1887 by Elkin Mathews and John Lane:

> Something approaching a craze for first editions was creating a
> market for new books by contemporary authors, especially books
> of belles-lettres issued in tastefully designed limited editions.[6]

J. H. Slater's *Early Editions* (1894) was the primer of this revolutionary change. In their account of resistance to this modern structure of book collecting, Carter and Pollard mention that one commentator accused Slater (who edited *Book Prices Current*, which he had founded in 1886) of catering to "the bric à brac collector" (104). Another attacked the first edition craze as "nothing more or less than barefaced gambling from beginning to end" (104, 105).[7] The main supporter of the modern school of book collecting was, of course, Thomas J. Wise (106).

John Carter was himself to expand on this history of book collecting in 1948, beginning his account with the establishment of the elementary apparatus of bibliophily across Europe in the seventeenth century.[8] He analyzes the transition to the modern in much more detail and as more than merely a change in the objects collected. For example, whereas early-eighteenth-century collectors "generally tended to think in terms of eventual public ownership of their books" (13), by museums or state libraries, by the end of the eighteenth century "a new conception was abroad," that of "the personal collection, which would either be kept in the family . . . or dispersed after the collector's own use and enjoyment of it" (14), the collection as private capital, so to speak. Using records of book sales, Carter was then able to mark with some precision the course of the further shift of "taste and technique" in collecting, first of all as moments "in the upward curve of the purely literary criterion in collecting taste" (18). Here I might remark that these changes did not simply occur in a developing transhistorical continuum (the "purely literary"); rather, they indicate the very constitution of this "purely literary" over time. Carter glosses the pioneering tastes of two American collectors, one of whom was collecting

Shelley first editions "at a date when such conduct must have been labelled eccentric," and the other who appears to have initiated the "cabinet" practice in book collecting, which prides itself on "a sort of microcosmic elegance, an ability to express a refined eclecticism within the confines of a single book-case" (19). Again, what is symptomatic in these collections is, first, the attention to the contemporary, and second, the manifestation, as microscopic elegance, of refined literary expression. Carter maintains that these two trends, a taste for *recent* first editions (or as Michael Sadleir put it, "the emergence of specific authors into 'first edition favour' ")[9] and an elegantly expressive collecting technique based on individual discrimination (60), were to meet in Locker-Lampson's Rowfant Library (1887). The Rowfant Library was further remarkable for first showing the other major factor in modern bibliophily, "the overriding importance attached to chronological priority—first edition, first issue, etc.—as a criterion of the interest of a book," for this now preponderant factor is a quite modern development (20). Wise, Buxton Forman, Slater, and others fostered the complementary development in bibliographical technique which I have mentioned, the modern author bibliography.[10] Wise, for example, provided in his bibliographies exactly what the rare book market needed, information on prices and comparative rarity. Because of these developments, "feverish and speculative conditions" (24) prevailed in the market, precisely the conditions in which a forger might flourish, since, as Carter shows, "the full-dress bibliography . . . incites the desire for completeness" (28).[11]

I have suggested that this whole process may be understood as an episode in the development of capitalist practices in the rare book trade; I want now to be more specific. What we may read here is the constitution of a particular capitalist structure of *value*. The value as commodities of books as physical objects is here being constructed in a particular way which will make its contribution to the discourse of "the literary" in the nineties and the early twentieth century. "Value" for the early modern collector is first of all value as *commodity*, i.e., as an object eventually to be exchanged, not to be removed from exchange to a library or museum. It is constructed both of "rarity," which is simply an exceptionality ensured by chronological priority, and of "completeness" in relation to some "sentimental," or personal, biographical criterion. Books are constructed as ideal commodities, as "perfect specimens of themselves," in Michael Sadleir's phrase; what is valuable is "a self-contained entity, with all its essential features and implications between its own covers."[12] In this way even a contemporary book might almost immediately attain "value," for value in books as physical objects was, since the nineties, a structure constituted by priority on as many scales as possible, along with some sentimental (i.e., arbitrary) "literary" relationship, or "association." These elements complement but also override those earlier values of tradition and skill of production sought after in the earlier manner of book collecting. It is significant that the chronological priority which creates "rarity" is relative only to a particular writer's *œuvre*, or to a particular text, for the *absolute* priority of straightforward age is devalued in the constitution of the modern book market. To valorize "age" as a criterion would be to close the market, a condition not acceptable under capitalism, in which the supply of commodities must be always expanding. So great was the desire to obtain early editions of popular authors, J. H. Slater wrote in 1894, "that a distinct trade has sprung up, not only for the purpose of ministering to the exigencies of the demand, but also to extend its scope."[13] The catalogue of Locker-Lamson's Rowfant Library, printed in 1886, for example, includes the first edition, in "original brown cloth," of Austin Dobson's *Proverbs in Porcelain and Other Verses*, which was published only nine years earlier.[14] The particular commodity which is the object of the modern collector's search is thus an arbitrary construct, taking its value from the market conditions created by the assumptions I have listed and by the bibliographers' specification of the "points" of a particular book, the modern discourse of "points" being also susceptible to corruption.[15]

I suggest that the "value" of a book as a physical object constructed out of these dialectical relations is one of the determinants of what was "literary value" in general in early modern England. The very "feverish," "speculative" conditions which invited the enterprise of Wise's forgeries of literary texts determined, along with other practices which are yet to be discussed, the discourse of "literary" value at the turn of the century. The practices of the modern market in rare books introduced and sustained particular ideologies of singularity and uniqueness as components of literary value, notions of the ahistorical arbitrariness of literary value certified by scholar-specialists, and notions of the personal, sentimental, or "humane" as appropriate to a literary commodity in a "democratic" social formation characterized by rules of market exchange. In *The Romance of Book-Collecting* (1898), Slater hints at the historical tension we have been exploring, between "list" and "enterprise," as he explains "the transition from the old to the new in the matter of books":

> a life of easy contentment engenders one mode of thought, a life of enterprise another; and the transition from the narrow limits of a prison-bound study to the open air is precisely what might have been expected to occur.[16]

The rare book trade was thus, I am arguing, one component within the larger structure of valorization of "the literary," determining the practices, entrepreneurial and list, of capitalist book production.

2. In *Book-Collecting: A Guide for Amateurs*, which he published in 1892, Slater listed among the resources of the collector *The Best Books*, by William Swan Sonnenschein, his own publisher. This work was a subject index of "best current books," giving prices, sizes, publishers' names, and first and last dates of publication, and it was consulted, said Slater, "by both dealers and amateurs."[17] But Swan Sonnenschein's "contribution towards classified bibliography" had first been published five years earlier, and it is the allusion which its title makes to its publishing context in 1887 which suggests another historical determination of "literary value." For that title was very self-conscious. Swan Sonnenschein wrote in his preface: "it has recently been shown that no two people agree as to even the 'Best Hundred Books'; and my lists do not profess to supply more than the titles of such as are universally regarded as good—absolutely and not relatively," and so he "endeavoured to interpret the word 'best' in its most catholic sense, applying it not only to books as to which a consensus of favourable opinion admittedly exists, but also to those which, even if not notably very good, have no betters."[18] This somewhat prickly negotiation by a publisher of the boundary between "the best" and "the good"—"the best in its most catholic sense"—points, in fact, to the issue in an important public debate among educators, critics, and journalists in the late eighties, the discussion over what was called "Sir John Lubbock's Hundred Best Books."

Sir John Lubbock, Baron Avebury, was a successful banker, an eminent natural scientist, and a reforming member of Parliament—the August bank holiday, known for a brief while as "St. Lubbock's Day," was one of his successes—when, in 1883, he succeeded Thomas Hughes as principal of F. D. Maurice's Working Men's College.[19] In his Principal's Address to the college in 1886, entitled "Books and Reading," Lubbock recommended to the students a list of "a hundred good books." The *Morning Advertiser* was the only daily newspaper to report his address, but it was republished (significantly with a "List of 100 Books" appended) as "On the Pleasure of Reading" in the *Contemporary Review* for February 1886, and as "The Choice of Books" in Lubbock's book of essays *The Pleasures of Life*.[20] This collection of essays went into a third edition by 1887 and Macmillan, its publisher, was still anticipating a large sale for Christmas 1889 (the Bodleian catalogue records an edition of the "204th thousand").[21] But an important, if small, change (similar to the appending of a list of "100") had been introduced to Lubbock's list of recommended books after the original, verbatim report in the *Morning Advertiser*: every subsequent reference to Lubbock's list and each successive revision refers, not to "a hundred good books," but to a "hundred *best* books." This particular change seems to have originated when the *Pall Mall Gazette* decided to popularize the list, for on the afternoon of the same day as the *Morning Advertiser*'s account of the speech, the *Pall Mall Gazette* published Lubbock's list of a hundred books[22] and invited various public figures, mainly men but including Lady Dilke (Mrs. Mark Pattison) and the novelists M. E. Braddon and Eliza Lynn Linton, to comment on Lubbock's selection. The responses were printed as they were received, as "The Best Hundred Books by the Best Hundred Judges," for the next four weeks, and then collected and republished in a "Pall Mall Gazette 'Extra'" in March 1886. I contend that this change from "good" to "best" is an important moment in the construction of the late Victorian ideology of literary value.

Lubbock wrote to the *Gazette* that he had purposely omitted

> (1) works by living authors, (2) science, and (3) history, with a very few exceptions [Herodotus, Thucydides, etc.], which I mentioned rather in their literary aspect. (12 January 1886, 2)

His original list included "Non-Christian Moralists," "Classics," "Epic Poetry," "Eastern Poetry," "Travels," "Philosophy," and "Greek Dramatists," as well as "Poetry and General Literature" and selections from "Modern Fiction." George Eliot, one of six novelists included, was the only woman named on the entire list. Henry James refused the invitation to comment; Oscar Wilde advised on "books not to be read at all" (none of John Stuart Mill except "On Liberty"—his comments were not reprinted in the "Extra"), and Ruskin recommended that "the best German books should at once be translated into French, for the world's sake, by the French Academy."[23] But what is more important is the reaction elsewhere to the *Pall Mall Gazette*'s publishing coup, the response of publishers and others in the press.

Although the *Saturday Review* objected that "reading should certainly be allowed to come by nature" and that "there is not much direct use, though there is a great deal of pleasant interest, in such a list as Sir John Lubbock offered for the approval of the Working-men's College,"[24] the publishers responded in a variety of ways. The language of their advertisements picked up those elements of the phrase "hundred best books" which best suited their current lists and plans. In the *Gazette* "Extra," for example, Mudie's proclaimed its "Constant Succession of All the Newest and Best Books" ("Extra" ii), while others promoted their own variations on "hundred best." Putnam's advertised "The Best Books" ("Extra" iv); Chatto, "Some of the Best Books" ("Extra" v). Ward Lock advertised its "New Popular Library of Literary Treasures" ("Extra" vi) ("ONE HUNDRED LITERARY TREASURES" proclaimed its ad in the *Publishers' Circular* for 1 April),[25] and Sampson, Low advertised *The Hundred Greatest Men* ("Extra" iv). In June, James Duffy and Sons of Dublin were advertising "some of the BEST HUNDRED BOOKS relating to Ireland" in the *Publishers' Circular*.[26] Other publishers simply repeated their own valorizing formulas, as in Routledge's "World Library" ("Extra" iv) or Cassell's "National Library" ("Extra" xi). The responses together suggest that there was perceived to be something unique and timely in the phrase "hundred best books." For, as Lubbock had been quick to acknowledge, there had been other lists of books recommended over the years, such as James Pycroft's *Course of English Reading* and James Baldwin's *The Book Lover* (both published in 1844 and reprinted often).[27] And a contemporary "Old Book Lover" had quickly reprinted in 1886 his own list from the *Sheffield Independent* as *The Best Books: A List for the Guidance of General Readers*, claiming that "several authors of the 'Lists of the Best Books,' which lately appeared in the *Pall Mall Gazette*, have been pleased to pronounce this list to be the most useful and comprehensive of any which have hitherto been published."[28] Macmillan, too, seized the opportunity to republish as the title essay of a collection Frederic Harrison's "The Choice of Books," a version of which had appeared in the *Fortnightly* in 1879.[29] The phrase "hundred best books," with variants, appears everywhere in 1886: "the hundred have swollen to more than four times the number, and the literature of all time seems put upon its trial," wrote "A Desultory Reader" in the *Leisure Hour*,[30] and the *Athenaeum* was moved to comment:

> We have lately had enough and to spare of the discussion promoted by Sir John Lubbock, and continued by the newspapers, as to the best hundred books, or whatever the number was.[31]

But the *Athenaeum*'s facetiousness about the number only points to the special character of Lubbock's "Hundred Best Books." If "An Old Book Lover," like Swan Sonnenschein in 1887, could see "no good reason for confining the number to one hundred,"[32] this was because the significance of the number was not arithmetical but ideological, signifying, as we shall see, attainable knowledge. Indeed, each term of the formula contributed to its distinctiveness, which has as its ultimate reference Matthew Arnold's idea of "culture." Arnold himself declined to comment to the *Pall Mall Gazette* on the "hundred best"; "Lists such as Sir John Lubbock's," he wrote, "are interesting things to look at, but I feel no disposition to make one" ("Extra" 23). But Professor Max Müller, in his response to the *Pall Mall Gazette* ("Extra" 17), pointed out that Arnold had contributed an introduction in 1879 to the poetry volume of a "Portrait Collection of the Hundred Greatest Men," published by Sampson, Low (an instance, R. H. Super claims, of "the nineteenth-century love of listing the 'greatest' in every category of human endeavour"). Arnold repeated the final paragraph of that introduction in his essay "The Study of Poetry," which itself originated as an introduction to T. H. Ward's *The English Poets* in 1880.[33] It was there, of course, that Arnold broached his theory of literary *touchstones*, arguing for keeping available for purposes of critical comparison "specimens of poetry of the high, the very highest, quality." Ironically, he also spoke in "The Study of Poetry" of how "religion has materialised itself in the fact," whereas "for poetry the idea is everything ... ; it attaches its emotion to the idea, the idea *is* the fact."[34] I say "ironically" because what I am tracing in the episode of "Lubbock's Hundred Best Books" is precisely the materialization of that idea of "culture" which underlies Matthew Arnold's whole critical project, "the best that has been thought and known in the world," a crucial formulation of "literary value" in the last half of the nineteenth century.[35]

It was the specificity of the formula "hundred best books," so irritating to some commentators, which appeared to fascinate both publishing entrepreneurs and the more conservative publishers. Coincident with the discussion of "the hundred best books," Cassell had published (at 6*d*. and 3*d*. a volume) its "New National Library," edited by Professor Henry Morley of London University. This was "the first of those 'libraries' through which [Morley] was to become known as the greatest *vulgarisateur* of literature of his age." [36] In welcoming this new series, the *Publishers' Circular* quoted from Cassell's press announcement Max Müller's approving comments:

> I am particularly glad to see that you do not mean to confine yourself to the so-called *Hundred Best Books*. Many of the best books are to be found among those that have but a small circle of friends.[37]

But soon a correspondence in the *Times*, reprinted in the *Publishers' Circular*, suggested that neither the "hundred best" nor any other version of the best that is known and thought was guiding the selection of Cassell's series. Henry Morley had previously been editing for Routledge a shilling series, "Morley's Universal Library," when he contracted to edit the new "National Library" for Cassell. Routledge claimed that Morley's new Cassell venture seemed simply to be reprinting his Routledge selections at one-fourth the price, and so in retaliation Routledge began publishing yet another series of the same books, a "World Library," at the same 3*d*. price but, according to Cassell, exactly one week before Cassell's announced dates of publication.[38] Clearly both publishers anticipated considerable profit from a series of books presented with "national," "world," "universal," or some other definitive authority. And since these were the market conditions into which intruded Lubbock's "Hundred Best Books," it is not surprising to see Lubbock, having been approached by Macmillan, who were doing so well with the original essay on the choice of books, instead accept, on 5 January 1890, £50 from George Routledge for "the general introduction and the sole right to use as a general title the words 'Sir John Lubbock's 100 Books,' so far as I can do so." [39]

As I have said, my interest in this story lies finally in the implications for the ideology of "value" in late Victorian publishing of Routledge's marketing "Lubbock's Hundred Books," making attainable as a commodity Matthew Arnold's "best that has been known and thought in the world." Routledge's hundred best books made up a series which radically challenged existing series, not only by the presumption of its "best," but by the exactness of its "hundred." For while the discussion in the *Pall Mall Gazette* tacitly authorized the assertion, *some* assertion, of a "best," the "best" under discussion were not "authors" or "thoughts" but *books*, material objects, indeed commodities. Moreover, once mooted, the convention was established that the series should number one hundred, a decimal which gestures toward comprehensiveness while asserting closure. As we have seen, Lubbock hedged on the assertion of "best" (originally being content with "good") and in his introduction to Routledge's series, he spoke of them as those books "most frequently mentioned with approval by those writers who have referred directly or indirectly to the pleasure of reading." He also hedged on the "hundred":

> Eleven books, or even thirty, would be very few; but no doubt I might just as well have given 90, or 110. Indeed, if our arithmetical notition [sic] had been duodecimal instead of decimal, I should no doubt have made up the number to 120. I only chose 100 as being a round number.[40]

"Round number" or no, the ideological setting of "one hundred" is clear. The phrase as a whole combines those aspirations for a "list" in which a publisher might take pride with the purposes of an enterprising publisher. The "hundred best" is a list which sells itself very effectively and rather more quickly than usual. Since one could always have bought a "select" book or a "world classic," unless a purchaser buys the whole "hundred" its "bestness" is not manifest. The prescription of a *hundred* "best" books thus completes the fetishization of "the classic." No longer the "undulating and diverse" relation to knowledge which Matthew Arnold prescribed, the "hundred best books" has an attainable completeness, a finality of its own, existing precisely as a fetish which may be owned. Thus publishers other than Routledge attempted to profit from this distinctive set of relations, this guarantee of attainable "literary value." Bohn advertised in the nineties a special library: since "many people have suggested that from Bohn a most attractive and valuable 'Best One Hundred Books' could easily be selected," they made a special offer, including a bookshelf "specially designed to hold the 100 Bohn Volumes." To accommodate the specific ideological advantages of a "hundred best books" to Bohn's traditional aim of including "everything," each purchaser was allowed to take either fifty or one hundred volumes, making their own choice from the whole Bohn list, although Bohn listed "a typical selection of 100 volumes . . . representative both of the different ages and the various countries of the world." [41]

Herodotus, the first volume of the Lubbock/Routledge "Hundred Books," was announced on 9 May 1891 in the *Publishers' Circular*, whose editors anticipated a large sale for the series—"of the value and practical importance of the series it is not necessary for us further to speak"—and the next volume, Darwin's *Voyage of a Naturalist*, was announced on 30 May. A new volume was to be added on the tenth and the twenty-fifth of each month, and by the time of the *Publishers' Circular*'s Christmas number in 1891 Routledge was able to advertise fifteen volumes in print. The advertisements in the 1894 Routledge volume, Locke's *On the Human Understanding*, lists seventy-five "best" books in print. It would appear from Routledge's records that the largest first printings were of *The Shi King: The Old "Poetry Classic" of the Chinese* and (despite Oscar Wilde) Mill's *Logic* (3,000 copies each), and the smallest first printing was of *Adam Bede* (208, with two subsequent runs of 104 copies each). Books in the series were reprinted at least until August 1898, and interest in "Lubbock's Hundred Best Books" persisted well into the twentieth century. In 1899, Harmsworth published a catalogue, *The 100 Best Books in the World of Literature as Selected by Sir John Lubbock, Bart.*, and in 1904 the *Pall Mall Gazette* tried to revive interest by announcing "Sir John Lubbock's (Lord Avebury's) New List." [42] Routledge was then encouraged to advertise in the 15 June *Pall Mall Gazette* that "a few sets of the Library are still available at the following prices":

> 100 volumes, neatly bound in Cloth, £9 net
> 100 volumes, strongly bound in Half Morocco, £10 net
> 100 volumes, very elegantly bound in best Lambskin, gilt, gilt tops, with silk registers, £12 net,

and there was a correspondence on the revised list for two weeks. [43] In 1917, W. Robertson Nicholl ("Claudius Clear") presented as "a library

for five pounds" a list of "the best books for reading, which shall include, say, one hundred volumes."[44]

Extending over thirty years, this discourse of a "hundred best books"
connected publishing practices with a particular reading—as *commodity*—of "the best that has been known and thought in the world."
A determinant discourse in this particular conception of "literary
value," it reduces (or expands) "the best" to its "hundred," and thence
to its own commercial purposes. Moreover, it interacts with the values
we have noticed in the contemporary rare book market. For example,
the particular version of "rarity" it promotes is a self-assured (because
"disinterested") "best"; its "best" is an arbitrary, conventional construct,
a "round number," authorized, as "uniqueness" and "priority" are
authorized in the rare book market, by experts who are familiar with
Herodotus, Locke, Confucius, Molière, and George Eliot and who can
thus ignore mere chronological, generic, or historical ("national") boundaries to arrive at a "best." As with the rare book market, which like
any market welcomes everyone with money, the selection of the "hundred best books" was "democratic," in that it was (among the experts)
consensual. Even the demurrer of, say, a Matthew Arnold was polite,
and as for the other "Best Judges," they merely recommended and accommodated. As his biographer records, "Sir John Lubbock believed
that his list was composed of books 'which everyone might read with
advantage,'" and when Ruskin condemned the "rubbish and poison"
which Lubbock had recommended, even that violence could be adjust-
ed to: "I confess," said Lubbock, "to being somewhat relieved when,
on looking through the books which he had struck out of my list, I found
they included, amongst others, Marcus Aurelius, Aristotle, Confucius,
Thomas à Kempis, Kingsley, Thackeray, Macaulay, and Emerson, so that
I hope I had not done so much harm, after all."[45] Sir John Lubbock,
polymath and public-spirited man, had performed a complicated task;
he had perceived that his original workingmens' audience needed, practically, guidance in the choice, not of ideas, but of *books*; he had thought
to present them with a good, round hundred. Confident that he would
not do "much harm," he was prepared to name the best. That this task
was also so commercially desirable he and others perceived only later,
and it was so only because of the general public acceptance, as *value*,
of the ideology of a "hundred best," making not only thinkable but
available for purchase "the best that has been known and thought in
the world."

3. Sir John Lubbock's Hundred Best Books, as I have mentioned, included the work of only one woman writer: "selections from George Eliot" ("Extra" 4). This, I should point out here, was Lubbock's "first list," compiled by the *Pall Mall Gazette* in January 1886, from the report of his lecture to the Working Men's College. To his "final list," published a month later in the *Contemporary Review*, Lubbock added "Miss Austen: Either 'Emma' or 'Pride and Prejudice' " ("Extra" 24); in his 1904 "Revised List," he again omitted, "with regret," and to the surprise of the editors, "Miss Austen's works," with the odd explanation that "English novels were, perhaps, over-represented."[46] Other than these changes, there is no indication of Lubbock's own, personal opinion of Jane Austen's work. Others among the "best judges," Lord Coleridge, M. E. Braddon, E. Lynn Linton, and Dr. J. C. Welldon, the headmaster of Harrow, had recommended Jane Austen, while Swinburne had included other women writers as well, E. B. Browning, Charlotte and Emily Brontë, and Elizabeth Gaskell, and Lady Dilke had added Madame de Staël, Madame de Sévigné, and Mrs. Craven. While there were clearly differing opinions over the relative value of the work of these women, none of the "best judges," nor anyone else, questioned the massive omission of women writers from all three of Lubbock's published lists of "the best." That this was nothing out of the ordinary in the 1880s is beside the point; I want to look at the structure of the "ordinary" in this case, that is, to enquire into the gender determinations of "the best," those relations which ensured that considerations of "literary value" at the turn of the century would always silently privilege the work of male writers, while always concealing that privileging by including George Eliot, or perhaps Jane Austen. Referring to my comments in the previous chapter on the work of Sylvia Walby, I should like to theorize this ideological structure as a "patriarchal/capitalist literary mode of production," by which I mean a particular articulation of the historical structures of patriarchy with the capitalist literary mode of production we have been describing. The task is made easier by the recent empirical and theoretical work of feminist writers. Annette Kuhn and Ann-Marie Wolpe for example, have insisted on the relationship between patriarchy and capital in general terms—"the precise character of the operation of patriarchal relations is shaped within the historical concreteness of a mode of production"[47]—but have not specified that shaping historically. I want now, acknowledging those patriarchal relations in paid work which

are used generally to retain women as unpaid laborers in the household, along with women's exclusion from education and from certain occupations, and their restriction to part-time occupations, to explore that exclusion specific to book production in the social construction of "literary value." Some feminists, notably Zillah Eisenstein, have pointed out that

> patriarchy (as male supremacy) provides the sexual hierarchical ordering of society for political control and as a political system cannot be reduced to its economic structure; while capitalism as an economic class system driven by the pursuit of profit feeds off the patriarchal ordering. Together they form the political economy of the society, not merely one or another, but a typical blend of the two.[48]

Sylvia Walby's interest not just in an "economic structure" but in "modes of production" and the articulation of relatively autonomous structures, and her analysis of the interaction of patriarchal relations with a particular system of capitalist relations (along with male violence and sexuality) as "a patriarchal mode of production," allow for a more precise historical description of late-nineteenth-century book production. As Walby says, patriarchal forms of exclusionary practice may be seen as a form of social closure: "They are both a product of, and themselves create, highly significant divisions among paid workers."[49] They are overdetermined by patriarchal divisions elsewhere in the social formation, and so from the earliest days of novel writing, women's work was differentiated and denigrated. Elaine Showalter describes in detail, as "forms of male resistance," the exclusionary practices casting women novelists as aggressive conspirators for male markets, or as incapacitated for good writing because of their physical deficiencies, limited experience, and emotionality.[50] G. H. Lewes, in 1852, claimed that women novelists excelled "in *finesse* of detail, in pathos and sentiment, while men generally succeed better in the construction of plots and the delineation of character."[51] What Sylvia Walby adds to this familiar story is a discussion of the *articulation* of patriarchal ideological practices with the practices of capitalist production. While "there is an extent to which the struggles around these practices have their own autonomy," the patriarchal mode of production has no "autonomous laws of development"; the capitalist mode of production with which the patriarchal mode is in articulation governs the nature of historical change.[52] Thus the articulation of patriarchy with the capitalist mode of production is one which allows essential difference within the closest interaction, patriarchy adapting its massive determinations to the historical development of the capitalist mode of production, as the capitalist mode of production incorporates the resistances of the patriarchal social formation. I want to see as a "patriarchal/capitalist literary mode of production" precisely the articulation (articulation as *interplay*) of the women's struggle over patriarchal publishing practices with the effort not only to establish a canon of "the best that has been known and thought" but also to define critically that "best" in a way that permits its commodification. The process, in other words, is truly dialectical, and the two moments of change in the sector of book production—patriarchal literary relations and the ideology of literary value—are each drawn on to produce a new patriarchal/capitalist ideology, which then dictates (or determines) the further development of each set of practices. Zillah Eisenstein chooses the phrase "capitalist patriarchy" to emphasize "the mutually reinforcing dialectical relationship between capitalist class structure and hierarchical sexual structuring."[53] I would argue in more historically specific terms that the capitalist literary mode of production, at this, the period of its consolidation, required hierarchies of *literary value*, national and generic canons, to be constituted. These embodied a consensus that "the best that has been known and thought" has a material (and potentially commercial) existence in "self-contained entities," and included even the most recent works, with all their essential features and implications between their own covers. At the same moment (or even at another) the patriarchal literary mode of production had always/already predetermined that these hierarchies be gendered.

Since the Education Act of 1870, the project of hierarchical ordering of cultural works might be said to meet a clear social need; Sir John Lubbock's address to the Working Men's College was only one of many attempts at guidance. And so, as we have seen, while the "best judges" might differ somewhat over the precise contents of his list, there was little debate over the appropriateness, indeed the need, for such a list in general. The differences over the admission/omission of Jane Austen, to stand (or curtsy) beside only George Eliot, signals that what informs this tacit consensus is, equally, *patriarchy*, that is, the necessity to enforce relations of male dominance. The production of literary texts was not a field of endeavor from which women in England were, or might be, excluded; there was already a body and tradition of women's writing, but within that tradition "division and differential status" were already enforced.[54] In the 1880s and 1890s, at the very time when "division and differential status" must be constituted as *general* structures of literary value, it was literally unthinkable that the existing structure of value which differentiated women's writing should not be powerfully determinant. The existence of a body of writing identified generally by theme and genre as "women's writing,"[55] by the very necessity that it be accounted for, determined that the capitalist literary mode of production, as it was being constituted, would be constituted as a *patriarchal*/capitalist literary mode of production. As Margaret Shaw demonstrates, reviewers "worked, wittingly or unwittingly, to 'construct' an image of the 'literate woman,' of her appropriate habits of reading and writing," so producing "an increased stratification of literacy which ultimately solidified and privileged the construction of a new 'man' of letters and his forms of literate behavior."[56] Again, G. H. Lewes' 1872 essay on Dickens builds upon an apparent aesthetic distinction "between show and Art, between 'fanciful flight' and Literature," but his language also demarcates "class and gender boundaries that preserve the dominant literary culture." As Jean Ferguson Carr remarks, "Lewes's articulation of the categories by which novels will be judged has been . . . durable."[57] But rather than itself being the cause or source, it is a symptom of the historical process. While determined by general patriarchal ideology, by the patriarchal mode of production (domestic labor) and other patriarchal relations, the patriarchal/capitalist literary mode of production was primarily the determinate effect of a specific, preconstituted ideological formation within a particular historical conjuncture, an instance again of structural causality. The moment of the consolidation of the ideology of literary value was determined by such market practices as we have examined earlier and by Arnold's powerful intervention on the ideological level. But it was at the same time necessarily a moment of division and differentiation, one which, as we have seen in the example of the Hundred Best Books, easily and silently accommodated the existing, autonomous patriarchal division and differentiation, generalizing and universalizing its patriarchal thematic and generic assumptions. As we shall see, the critical debate over "realism" and "romanticism" from the 1870s to the 1890s was set amongst these questions. In part a rediscovery and promotion of romance by male authors such as Robert Louis Stevenson "against a background of Zolaism—or Jamesism," [58] the debate reveals its patriarchal determinations both in its silence about women writers of romances and in what is said: a work of art, Stevenson humbly remonstrated, "is neat, finite, self-contained, rational, flowing and emasculate." [59] Thus it is unhistorical to claim that "only women novelists ... have been brought into disrepute for their supposed popular appeal, their penchant for petty romance, and their consequent debasement of literature." [60] While women writers were indeed so treated, the literary values which these judgments assume, while they were forged in the struggle over women's writing, become, in the patriarchal/capitalist literary mode of production at the turn of the century, the universalized values which can discriminate not only against women's writing but against *any* writing which falls short of "the best." As Eleanor Marx and Edward Aveling pointed out: "To cultured people, public opinion is still that of man alone, and the customary is the moral." [61] The Victorian critical "double standard," [62] it might be said, is transmuted into a single standard, "literary value," while never for a moment losing its duplicity as regards women's writing, as in Lubbock's "English novels were, perhaps, over-represented." While enforcing judgments and canons which are objectively gender-determined, the standards of division and differentiation are themselves apparently ungendered. For example (to anticipate), from that standpoint Arnold Bennett might be (and was) dismissed for his popular appeal and his penchant for petty romance, his finesse of detail, his pathos and sentiment, and Stevenson was a writer of boy's books.

From this standpoint it is mistaken to read the history of women novelists in relation to men novelists as a direct linear development, to suggest that the general patriarchal ideology of the whole social formation dictated that women novelists be somehow overwhelmed by male novelists from the 1840s onward, that "men began to define the high-culture novel as a male preserve" and "began to edge women out of literature." To speak of a male "invasion" (even as an invasion of "an empty field") in the mid-nineteenth century, followed by a "redefinition" of the "good" novel in the 1880s and 1890s, and finally an "institutionalization" of the male hold on the "high-culture novel" in the early years of this century, [63] is to reduce to purposeful action, involving clear-cut objectives and equally clear-cut objects, what is a dialectical, that is, complexly interactive, struggle, one that is ultimately determined by developments in the material production of books over the whole nineteenth century. As Margaret Shaw points out, for example,

> various reviewers, including both men and women, devised con-
> structions of female literacy which, while serving separate ends, had
> the effect of consolidating and then preserving a politically elite
> definition of literacy that supported a particular gender and class.[64]

The "high-culture novel" was not simply an object or terrain to be fought for during those years; that very distinction, "high culture novel," and ones like it, were constructed only out of the processes of division and differentiation we have been describing: the interplay, or overlap, of the desire for the best novels as material objects, with the traditional patriarchal necessity to differentiate and subordinate the female. "Male dominance" was not simply "institutionalized"; rather a patriarchal/ capitalist ideology of "literary value" was constituted and a canon was established by the material practices of literary criticism, awards, and anthologies, and of lists like Lubbock's.

Theorizing, or visualizing, this articulation of patriarchy and the capitalist literary mode of production not simply as an evolution, or even, mechanistically, as a simple addition, but as an *overlaying*, as an "imbrication," of two autonomous historical moments, producing what Fredric Jameson calls a "layering or sedimentation," "the domi-nant structure of the classical modernist text,"[65] allows us to under-stand the "ordinariness" of the silence surrounding the patriarchalism of Lubbock's Hundred Best. To discriminate systematically a "hundred best," to establish a canon, would be necessarily to exclude many women writers, but to do this the criteria would be thought to be universal criteria. The judgment of women's writing became an ele-ment of the judgment of writing generally, a silent determinant of "literary value." Thus when the American critic Brander Matthews, writing on "Cheap Books and Good Books" for a British audience in 1891, stated that "the cheap books to be bought in the United States are only too often the trivial trash of the ladies who call themselves 'Ouida' and 'The Duchess,' "[66] his readers would recognize the right-ness of his dismissal of "ladies' trash" at the same time as they recog-nized its clinching appropriateness in a discussion of literary value in general.

4. Brander Matthews' remarks on "ladies' trash" were part of a contribution he made to the widespread discussion from the seventies onward of the desirability of international copyright. Matthews was attempting to make a general point from the American experience of the absence of international copyright. The opponents of international copyright, he writes, who

> do not wish to deprive the poor boy of the cheap book he may study by the firelight after his hard day's work, would perhaps be surprised to be told that of the "Hundred Best Books" (of which we lately had so many lists), of the books best fitted to form character and to make a man, very few indeed, not more than half a dozen, are to be found in any of the cheap libraries which flourish because of the absence of copyright. Most of these great works are old and consecrated by time; they are nearly all free to be printed by those whoso will. In Sir John Lubbock's original list of a hundred best authors only two were American, and only twelve were recent Englishmen whose works are still protected by English copyright.[67]

That Matthews forgets Lubbock's expressed exclusion of living writers from his list does not, perhaps, entirely destroy his point, that the connections between copyright, public taste in books, and literary quality are not simple and direct. While the absence of an international copyright convention did not *foster* "good" books, copyright would not seem, on the other hand, to be an obstacle to the distribution of the good, or even the "best," for the connection between quality and price would seem to be socially, even geographically, determined: "In America, the cheapest books are not good books, for the most part; certainly they are not the best books. *In Europe the best books are the cheapest*" (354). While only a few would have argued a direct correlation between national market, copyright, and literary quality, Matthews' point had a popular appeal, especially, as we shall see, to the exponents of "free trade." Here I want to examine those dimensions of place and time in the constitution of ideologies of literary value, especially in relation to the efforts, in the final quarter of the nineteenth century, to institute international copyright.

International copyright law originated in the French revolutionary laws of 1791 and 1793, which made no distinctions among authors whose rights were protected in France and freely granted French copyright to foreign works. But only Belgium, in the ensuing years, followed the revolutionary French example of unilateral protection of works published abroad. Yet the number of bilateral agreements between individual European states, dealing particularly with translation rights, grew in the first half of the nineteenth century, until by 1886 only Greece, Monaco, some of the Balkan states, and Asian and American states, including the United States, were without any international copyright agreements. But while the network of bilateral copyright arrangements prior to 1886 was extensive, the protection which this offered to authors in countries other than their own was neither comprehensive nor systematic.[68] The pressure for a universal law of copyright, however, arose less out of a desire for juridical consistency than from the material contradictions of time and place for which "modernism" was the resolution on the ideological level. This can be seen in the events leading up to the Berne Convention of 1887.

In September 1858, a Congress on Literary and Artistic Property was held in Brussels which passed resolutions constituting "a rudimentary outline of a programme for a universal copyright law," and in 1878, during the Paris Exhibition, the French Société des Gens de Lettres held an international literary congress, presided over by Victor Hugo. This congress passed further resolutions on international copyright and founded an International Literary Association to protect literary property and to organize regular relations between literary societies and writers of all countries. Over the next few years, the ALI held annual congresses, and it persuaded the Swiss government in 1883 to sponsor a conference in Berne for "the formation of a Union of literary property." This conference produced the draft of a "universal literary convention," which became the basis for the successful negotiations between governments at the Berne Diplomatic Conferences of 1884, 1885, and 1886.[69] In the meantime, the British Parliament had passed, in 1837 and 1844, successive acts to protect in the United Kingdom books and other artistic works imported from those countries which afforded a reciprocal protection to British publications. By 1886, copyright agreements had been established by Orders in Council with sixteen European states. As the negotiations proceeded in Berne in the eighties, Britain, a participant at the conferences, passed in anticipation the International Copyright Act of 1886, which empowered the queen to issue Orders in Council embodying the chief features of the new convention. The United States, on the other hand, had sent only observers to the Berne conferences, and, while never joining the convention, passed the "Chace Act" in 1891, which granted copyright to authors of certain specific nationalities (including British subjects), whose work was first, or simultaneously, published, or "manufactured," in the United States.[70]

The forces driving the multilateral initiatives toward international copyright are perhaps not immediately clear. Nor does the "jocular" label piracy, meaning simply "free-booting with reference to literary property,"[71] provide a sufficient explanation; "piracy," as Brander Matthews wrote, "is a term available for popular appeal but perhaps lacking in scientific precision,"[72] since most countries, while they protected works by their own authors, did not regard the unauthorized publication of foreign works as unfair or immoral.[73] The exigencies of book production in the eighties and nineties were the determining factors in the pressure for international copyright. In his evidence before the Royal Commission on Colonial and International Copyright in 1876, Sir Charles Trevelyan made two statements which he presented as universal truths but which clearly gesture toward the most broad historical pressures. Distinguishing the author's own pecuniary interest in his work from that of his publishers, Trevelyan said:

> the interest of the author consists simply in the remunerative sale of his works anywhere and everywhere, it matters not by whom, provided he gets his fair remuneration. But the interest of the publisher is quite different, it is local.

And in the same testimony, Trevelyan remarked: "it is of great consequence that books should reach the body of the people fresh and fresh"; a recently published book might be good, even "a classic," but its goodness would be enhanced, Trevelyan's archaism emphasizes, if it were "not deteriorated or changed by lapse of time: not stale, musty or vapid."[74] Trevelyan does not seem aware of his own assumption about the contradiction between ubiquity and locality, or those in his notion of literary "freshness," yet it is precisely these conflicting conceptions of space and time which are the larger determinations of the debate over international copyright. For example, it was said to be a general feeling in the United States that international copyright was simply a scheme whereby British publishers might capture the American book market, yet it was obvious that any British publisher, even after 1891, "had to calculate cost, freight charges, insurance and import duty before deciding whether the American international copyright act was in any way beneficial to a particular book." [75] Whereas earlier conflict around copyright in England could be said to have been determined, literally, by an insularity which confined the issues to the nature of a book or text and how that might most profitably be exploited in an English market, the constraints of English space and (so to speak) Greenwich time had, by the late nineteenth century, been superseded, since "modernism" (we are talking here about the general ideological level of the capitalist social formation) takes as one of its missions "the production of new meanings for space and time." [76]

Railways, transatlantic steamships, and telegraphy are only the most obvious instances of the material pressures for new meanings for space and time in early modern book production. Simply to consider *space* raises concrete questions of domicile and nationality, whether of author or of publisher, questions of the different kinds of geopolitical border, not only the Atlantic Ocean or the English Channel, but the long Canadian-American land boundary. Augustine Birrell, for example, wrote with mock querulousness about the Canadian "piracy" of English books for the American market:

> So far as the United States was concerned our authors had no remedy but abuse—but Canada, was it not, as it were, our own kail-yard? Did not the Queen's writ run there and so on? [77]

And J. A. Froude wondered who could collect the sort of minimal royalty that was suggested as a "free trade" alternative to copyright in different countries under different governments. [78] Again, there was the problem of sheer geographical size in organizing existing or potential markets. As one American wrote:

> Your Mudie can mail books at a cheap rate to subscribers in every part of the United Kingdom, and get them back from the farthest limit within a week or ten days. But a Boston or New York library could not lend books to subscribers in Nevada or Dakota, thousands of miles away. [79]

The size of the United States, and its sociopolitical and ideological divisions, engaged the question of copyright in yet another way:

two years since certain persons in the West—publishers of Chicago
and St Louis—vindicated for themselves the original freedom of
citizens of the United States to reprint the works of Englishmen,
and they reduced their prices to make a market. . . . The publishers
of Chicago threatened to destroy the trade of the publishers of New
York. . . . At present the publishers of the older cities are principally,
if not solely, affected, and it is they who have made the discovery
that the question of international Copyright has become "pressing." [80]

Similarly, international copyright dictated that the dimension of
time was no longer to be structured simply as *duration*, the length of
copyright and its relation to an author's lifetime which would allow
him or her a fair reward and produce a profit for the publisher. Further-
more, not only "freshness" but staying power (or "shelf life") was a commercial value; J. A. Froude argued: "Books of real worth survive the
copyright period, and, the verdict of continued demand being finally
passed, they carry with them their own commendation and become
the property of the public." [81] Unprecedented speedy communication
not only could "boom" a book but could introduce pressures on the
time another book might have to become a critical and financial success. And, politically, issues of *precedence* of date of publication, or alternatively of *simultaneity*, were crucial. For time and space were often in-
timately connected in copyright law: after the "Chace Act," a book
needed to be published in both countries simultaneously to conform
with both U.S. and British copyright law, although later measures were
adopted to grant *ad interim* copyright for a book first published abroad
while it was being manufactured in the United States, [82] and not even
an author's twelve-month residence in the United States could earn
copyright protection for a work without its author obtaining U.S.
citizenship. [83]

The Berne Convention and the international copyright legisla-
tion which preceded it restructured the accepted understandings of
time and space in the interest of capitalist publishing. The convention established a "union," ensuring reciprocity in the treatment of
authors, or most often, publishers—"their lawful representatives"—
within the signatory nations, so that they would "enjoy in other countries for their works, whether published in one of those countries or
unpublished, the rights which the respective laws do now or may hereafter grant to natives." The Berne Convention established:

> The country of origin of the work is that in which the work is
> first published, or if such publication takes place simultaneously
> in several countries of the Union, that one of them in which the
> shortest term of protection is granted by law;

and

> The enjoyment of these rights . . . cannot exceed in the other coun-
> tries the term of protection granted in the said country of origin.[84]

The spatial dimensions of copyright, and the temporal, and their interaction, were thus recast. What characterizes this early modern social
reconstruction of space and time in book production and distribution
is, in fact, the reduction of space (place of publication, nationality of
author, etc.) to a category contingent on time (time of publication, duration of property rights, etc.), a change which facilitates the rapid turnover of capital. The old forms of spatialization in publishing inhibited
processes of change, simply underwriting the timelessness of, say, a publisher's "list," or of the "hundred best books," in the face of entrepreneurial publishing practices. To establish the precedence of time over
space in publishing, as the Berne Convention did, was to valorize not
only "timing" but Trevelyan's unspoiled "fresh and fresh," what Froude
less enthusiastically called the "prevailing and passing delirium,"[85] so
as to hasten capital turnover. As David Harvey argues, "Those who
define the material practices, forms, and meanings of money, time or
space fix certain basic rules of the social game," and the rules fixed by
the Berne Convention overcame those spatial barriers and temporal
understandings which impeded the turnover of publishing capital. The
institutional context was thus established for "literary" values, which
came to be associated with, for instance, the best-seller, in competition with fixed investments in publishing "lists." "The incentive to
create the world market," Harvey writes,

> to reduce spatial barriers, and to annihilate space through time is
> omni-present. . . . Innovations dedicated to the removal of spatial
> barriers . . . have been of immense significance in the history of
> capitalism, turning that history into a very geographical affair.[86]

The debate in Britain at the time of the Royal Commission on
Copyright, 1875–76, presented just these issues in its entrenched posi-

tions. The commission included among its members Fitzjames Stephen, and in its second year, J. A. Froude and Anthony Trollope, but the commissioners whose participation best reveals the issues were the civil servants from the Board of Trade, Sir Louis Mallett and Thomas Henry Farrer: in an article in the *Edinburgh Review*, Froude called the controversy over international copyright "the battle of the Board of Trade."[87] Both commissioners from the Board of Trade were doctrinaire free-traders: Mallett ("a Cobdenite *pur sang*," according to a friend)[88] was, after Cobden's death, "the chief official representative of free trade opinion,"[89] and Farrer, permanent secretary to the Board of Trade, was "a free-trader of unyielding temper" who was by far the most powerful member of the inquiry. The *DNB* speaks of his "unseen and quiet influence," which was so effectual that "between 1872 and 1886 almost all the reforms of and additions to our system of commercial law were only brought about with the concurrence of the secretary of the board of trade."[90] Farrer was not to be so influential in the matter of copyright, and the circumstances of his defeat are historically significant. He did not sit on the inquiry during its second session, in 1876, but he appeared as a witness five times, was thoroughly interviewed by Mallett, and on his final appearance he was asked to submit a written summary of his evidence and suggestions.[91] Like Mallett, Farrer saw free trade as "merely the unshackling of powers which have an independent existence":

> All it can do, and that all is much, is to leave the powers of nature and of man to produce whatever it is in them to produce unchecked by human restrictions.[92]

And, again like Mallett, he asserted that a literary work produced by men and women with little or no copyright privileges would somehow be a "better" work. At times during the inquiry, Mallett's questions were so doctrinaire that, for instance, the publisher John Blackwood, called as a witness, simply could not understand him; when Mallett asked Blackwood about extending "the area of consumption and of profit" while reducing "the term of protection" so as to "obtain the same results in stimulating authors to their best efforts," Blackwood, balking at "the sort of abstract question," simply answered: "I cannot follow that."[93] While Farrer was more subtle in his presentation of the logic of political economy, even Herbert Spencer, another witness, considered Farrer's references to the unrestrained issue of rival editions as "free trade" and his habit of calling copyright "monopoly" to be "question-begging."[94] Locked in his abstract categories, Farrer persistently argued for a tight restriction on "the abstract principle of monopoly" in copyright, saying that the ideal copyright system "should be co-extensive with the English language, giving the author the benefit of an enormous market and the reader the benefit of a price proportionately reduced."[95] He claimed, like Mallett, that free trade in books would improve the quality of literary production: "on the whole we must trust to the public demand purifying itself."[96] When Fitzjames Stephen asked him if the remuneration of English authors should be increased, he stipulated, "good English authors," although he agreed that there could not be any "definite or assignable relation between the money payment made to an author and the permanent value of his book." And under pressure from Stephen over his attempt to distinguish "good" authors, Farrer simply reasserted the free trade logic of his position, that "the author's remuneration must depend upon the public demand for his book."[97]

Only Mallett and Farrer attempted to make a case before the Commission of Inquiry that laws of international copyright would influence the quality or value of the literary works produced. As Froude said:

> The movement against copyright has originated with, and been carried on by, two or three speculative gentlemen in a Government department, who cannot reconcile the existing book trade with the orthodox theory of the nature of *value*.[98]

Fitzjames Stephen's cross-examination made it clear that their case was founded only on abstract political economic opinions about what might be "good" or "very rubbishy" in literature, based on analogy to the production of simple commodities.[99] After the commission's report, Farrer wrote in the *Fortnightly* (in a sort of confused rebuttal of the Arnoldian view of "the literary") that the "essence of a book" lies in the "facts" or "ideas" it contains, rather than in its "form" or arrangement of these facts, whereas copyright law protects not the "facts" but the "form of words":

> Original thought and observation, the highest form of mental labour, go unprotected, whilst literary manufacture, a very inferior product of the intellect, alone obtains protection.[100]

Copyright has thus "a tendency to encourage bad writers at the expense of good ones," wrote Farrer; "it tends to make books bad, numerous and dear." [101] But what the insular, outmoded free trade discourse of Sir Louis Mallett and T. H. Farrer could not accommodate, and what over-rode their opposition, were the concrete spatial and temporal particu-larities of the book trade at the turn of the century. When Farrer speaks of an ideal copyright system, "co-extensive with the English language," he ignores the historical determinations of any such system; indeed, while he means to encourage the "extension" of the market for books, his allusion to "the English language" is in fact parochial, recalling the island language rather than its concrete, historical (not to say imperial) extensions beyond geographical, social, and political boundaries, and its interaction with foreign languages. To create a world market in English books required the reduction of *spatial* (not just "trade") bar-riers. The doctrines of free trade had become, by the seventies and eighties, so abstract, so removed from social and economic practice, that the Royal Commission on Copyright, for all the confusion and disagreement in its report, rejected unequivocally a free trade in books which excluded international copyright, despite the influence exerted by the free trade dogmatists of the Board of Trade. Simplistic ideologies of supply and demand could not dictate to the modern market in books, however much they might dictate a particular ideology of literary value. International copyright, in fact, structured a new, world market for English books whose ideologies of value must accommodate the work of not only familiar local writers, of whatever locality, but also foreign writers—indeed, of "international" writers. The International Con-gresses of Publishers, in the nineties, were to propose, as we have seen, "codes of usages" for such a new world market.

By the nineties the ideologies of "literary value" encompassed not only the traditional but the very recent, not only the exceptional but the "personal" association, not only the "best" but the accessible or attainable. Moreover, this ideological formation engaged time-honored patriarchal critical discriminations against emotionality, fineness of detail, and petty romance, just as it admitted both the local and the foreign, or international. These and other criteria of literary value were enforced by contemporary material practices. I want now to consider briefly how these interact with the distinctive structures of capitalist publishing. I have referred to the ideologies of "literary value" as a "structure of valorization," emphasizing that it is a structure, an interplay of moments, and that its interaction with the structures of publishing is again various and complex, overdetermined. Any one of the positions comprehended in the ideologies of value we have been considering would interact with the practices of entrepreneurial and list publishers differently. However much (or little) any particular list publisher might construct their list so as to engage "traditional" concepts of literary value, an enterprising publisher would do so less; similarly, the personal, biographical associations of a new book would be valued more highly by the entrepreneur than by the list publisher (unless, perhaps, a new book on Byron, say, were submitted to John Murray). A list publisher would be more inclined to admit a "hundred best" than would an entrepreneur, once the "nonce value" had been realized by Routledge in publishing Lubbock's list as a set. Enterprising and list publishers might tend to value differently finely detailed romances, not to say "ladies' trash," just as the opportunities presented by an international copyright agreement might differ, depending on whether you habitually "boomed" best-sellers or tried to publish "books that will live." But I want to go further: not only did the determinant structures of literary value develop different effectivities out of such material practices as I have examined, but in the major theoretical debates of the time on the novel, such categories as "realism" and "romance," or "art" and "popular," were defined and fixed by these same material structures of value. In the eighties, Walter Besant, Henry James, and Robert Louis Stevenson debate these categories, and their arguments show a determinate relationship to the practices of entrepreneurial and list publishers, as well as to these specific ideologies of literary value. And so I want now to examine their work closely, turning afterward to the very different conjuncture and the very different novels of Hall Caine, Marie Corelli, and Arnold Bennett.

3. The Process of Literary Capital in the 1880s

Besant, James, and Stevenson

THE public debate about "the art of fiction" carried on by Walter Besant, Henry James, and Robert Louis Stevenson in 1883–84 is the occasion around which I want to build my discussion in this chapter; that, and a novel by each writer written at that time: Besant's *All Sorts and Conditions of Men* (1883–84), James's *The Princess Casamassima* (1885–86), and Stevenson's *Strange Case of Dr. Jekyll and Mr. Hyde* (1886). The conjuncture of the three statements on fiction provides only the most tenuous, flexible link between the ideological work of the three writers, flexible enough to accommodate my analyses of their three very different places within capitalist publishing (or the tension between "list" and "entrepreneurial") and of their very different textual practices. On 25 April 1884, Walter Besant, a popular novelist (until 1884 his novels were written in collaboration with James Rice) who had, since September 1883, been organizing what was to become the Society of Authors, delivered a lecture at the Royal Institution entitled "The Art of Fiction." Henry James responded in the September *Longman's Magazine* with his own "Art of Fiction," and Stevenson commented on both with "A Humble Remonstrance" in *Longman's* in December. Mark Spilka points out, in the essay in which he places these three statements in the context of what James called "an era of discussion," that, "technically," the discussion in England of fiction as an art had begun in 1882 with William Dean Howells' essay "Henry James, Jr." in the *Century Magazine* and Stevenson's "A Gossip on Romance" in *Longman's*.[1] But there are, as we know, material "contexts" to all these texts as well, conditions of their production, including diverse ideological conditions, which would determine their different ideological effects. Thus I want to escape the "technicalities," the controversies over the "art of fiction" read intertextually on their own aesthetic level. I shall instead read the writing of each of the three writers symptomatically, as each exemplifying theoretically and in novelistic practice certain historical discourses of literary value within the different and contradictory structures of eighties publishing, making new connections through their material history. I shall begin with a reading of Besant's essay, and then of his novel.

1. Mark Spilka characterizes Walter Besant as simply "an amiable fool" who "set James going," whose lecture on the art of fiction was full of loosely spaced lunacies, like his later work *The Pen and the Book* (1891), which Mark Twain refused to review because there wasn't "a rational page in it." But rather than dismiss it as "mindless babble," mocking the absence of "reason" in it, we might look for the reason *of* "The Art of Fiction": what were the precise determinations of Besant's talk to the Royal Institution, the conditions of its possibility? If Besant "held in half-baked solution the whole swirl of received ideas about fiction,"[2] what produced that particular solution? I would suggest, in the first place, *venue*. Besant was speaking before an organization which had been founded in 1799 to "teach the application of science to the useful purposes of life."[3] When the institution's prospectus was revised under Faraday's influence in 1851–52 to encourage research in "pure" science, its primary aim was then restated as " 'to promote Science and Literary research' (literary having the connotation of 'learned' rather than its modern specialized meaning)."[4] It was primarily these institutional reasons, not Besant's inadequacies, which made Professor James Dewar's "Discourse" on low-temperature research and the liquefaction of gases the Royal Institution's most memorable lecture in 1884, rather than Besant's "Art of Fiction."[5] Moreover, the venue determined the attitude toward fiction in Besant's lecture, as in his three initial "propositions" about fiction: "that Fiction is an Art in every way worthy to be called the sister and the equal" of the Fine Arts; "that it is an Art which, like them, is governed and directed by general laws"; and that unlike the more mechanical arts, "no laws or rules whatever can teach it to those who have not already been endowed with the natural and necessary gifts." The venue also determined the "rules" and "principles" which he laid out in a fairly orderly way: to write from experience, and to ensure clarity in characterization, a conscious moral

purpose, and beauty of workmanship.[6] Since "for every Art there is the corresponding science which may be taught" (28), Besant spoke to the Royal Institution of the "science" corresponding to the art of fiction. The "general laws," "rules," and "principles" are not simply things that "Besant was fond of";[7] they compose Besant's essay in the science of fiction writing. As Bruce McElderry said of the essay: "It is simple but not really simple-minded."[8]

Besant's reference to "the newly founded Society of Authors" (27) indicates another ideological determination of his "Art of Fiction":

> it was in the month of September and the year 1883 that a small company of twelve or fifteen men met in Mr. Scoones's chambers, Garrick Street, in order to form an association or society of men and women engaged in letters.[9]

In the Royal Institution lecture, Besant mentions only his hope that the new Society of Authors might advise young writers of fiction, but his preoccupation with the *social* context of authorship suffuses the lecture. As John Goode put it, "Besant was lecturing as the unofficial spokesman of what was felt to be an important movement in the literary world."[10] Declaring fiction to be one of the fine arts, he does not go on to analyze the nature of fiction. Rather, he discusses the status, or the social "level," of fiction writers in late Victorian society, "the general—the Philistine—view of the Profession" (6), the one held by "the multitudes by whom a novelist has never been considered an artist at all" (4):

> Consider for a moment how the world at large regards the novelist. He is, in their eyes, a person who tells stories, just as they used to regard the actor as a man who tumbled on the stage to make the audience laugh, and a musician as a man who fiddled to make the people dance. (5)

Unlike practitioners of the other Arts and Sciences, novelists did not receive "their share of the ordinary national distinctions" (5). Spilka comments here that Henry James had at that time received even less public honor than Walter Besant,[11] but this is to reduce Besant's point to a concern about relative *individual* prestige, whereas "it is for its attitude towards the *profession* that Besant criticizes the public."[12] Besant is speaking here of the condition of writers generally, as artists, just as in his direction of the Society of Authors and, after 1890, in his "conducting" of the *Author*, he is interested in particular authors' cases as mainly *exemplary*, as indicating the status of the profession and its relations with publishers. Besant worries that the "class" of writers does not hold "annual exhibitions, dinners, or conversazioni," is not "associated" (5). The founding of the Society of Authors, he clearly thought, might help to correct this, and his aspirations for the society tacitly support his overall attitude in "The Art of Fiction" toward writers as a group.

Besant (that is, his lecture) was "a register for the national mind," joining new commonplaces to old ones;[13] it is a register of commonplace and often contradictory social and aesthetic ideologies in 1884. Thus it is less significant that he valued highly Blackmore's *Lorna Doone* or James Payn's *Confidential Agent* than that his preferences derive from ideologies of literary value that make it inevitable that he should admire those works. The symptom of Besant's ideological position is less his addled values than the complacency with which they are asserted. He claims that Payn's *Confidential Agent* shows, "if I may be permitted to say so, constructive power of the very highest order" (29), and the significant point is less his critical misjudgment than the tacit permission, the contented acquiescence, which he assumes in his hearers. The particular values which underpin his judgment of Payn are indeed banal (they would fit easily into the discussion of the "Hundred Best Books" in 1886), but more important they are assumed to be shared with his hearers. "To the unpractised hand," he writes,

> it would seem as if stories of theft [such as Payn's] had already been told *ad nauseam*. The man of experience knows better: he knows that in his hands every story becomes new, because he can place it upon his stage with new incidents, new conditions and new actors. (29)

The "man of experience" is, of course, not only James Payn but Walter Besant, novelist. But it is also, to some extent, as the anticlimax of his "better" knowledge demonstrates, each member of Besant's audience at the Royal Institution. In *Confidential Agent*, James Payn's "new conditions" would seem to be, surprisingly, "three or four quite ordinary families." Payn "does not search for strange and eccentric characters," says Besant, "but uses the folk he sees around him, plain middle-class people, to whom most of us belong" (29). The conjoining of "quite ordinary" with "plain middle-class" is authorized by Besant's self-satisfied invoking of "most of us," complacently conceding a remnant which, looking around the lecture hall, Besant would see did not really exist. Besant's specific comments on Payn exhibit everywhere this same complacency. Payn does not try to show his characters

> cleverer, better cultured, or in any respect at all other than they really are, except that some of them talk a little better than in real life they would be likely to do. (29)

The repeated, unself-conscious, "realistic" circularity of Besant's judgments enacts in their periods, so to speak, the class complacency he knows his audience to share.

These same characteristics show themselves in all the "laws," "principles," and "propositions" in Besant's lecture to the Royal Institution: a positivist or scientistic empiricism, a nascent "professional" militancy, and a middle-class complacency; these might be said to structure his "authorial ideology." For example: "The very first rule in Fiction is that the human interest must absolutely absorb everything else" (10). Besant demonstrates this "scientific" rule by the artistic practice of Charles Reade, "this great Master of Fiction" (a *status* rather than a description), by referring to Reade's description, "in his incomparable tale of the 'Cloister and the Hearth,'" of a journey through France:

> so great is the art of the writer, that, almost without being told, we see the road, a mere rough track, winding beside the river and along the valleys; we see the silent forests where lurk the *routiers* and the robbers, the cut-throat inn, the merchants, peasants, beggars, soldiers who go riding by; the writer does not pause in his story to tell us of all this, but yet we feel it—by the mere action of the piece and the dialogue we are compelled to see the scenery. (10)

And we not only see these strangers, but through our "modern Sympathy" (Besant's "essentially class-orientated faith," says John Goode),[14] we "understand their very souls" (11–12). Not only does Besant here assume the value of what can only be called "the preconstituted" (since it is presented with "the fewest possible of words" [10]) in the experience of a fiction, but he assumes as well the concurrence of his audience in his valuation. Restating his "rule," he says, "The human interest in Fiction, then, must come before aught else. It is of this world, wholly of this world" (10), and this world which he invokes with such assurance is a simple empiricist world; Besant says that the writer should keep a notebook "so that nothing is lost" (21), a phrase that Henry James was to transform. But Besant's world is also one in which writers are to be granted the status of "great Master" and a world in which we all, with minimum assistance, and in the lecture hall of the Royal Institution, may see the sights and persons of fifteenth-century France.

Besant's critics, from R. H. Hutton to Mark Spilka, take exception to another one of his "rules" for novelists: "never to go beyond your own experience" (16). But the contradiction which the critics light upon is symptomatic of a blindness rather than of some omitted mode of experience: it does not suffice for Hutton to extend the boundaries of experience to include the imagination, for "experience," after all, can never be "full." The significant inclusions and exclusions of "experience" are ideological. Besant, for example, while he mentions Tartuffe (19) and the *Comédie Humaine* (12), includes only one foreign writer, Victor Hugo, in a list of "great Masters of the Art" (35), while Hawthorne is included in another list of works "which are acknowledged to be of the first rank in fiction" (29). Besant's examples of a writer's "experience" are limited by his very British assumptions—and by his assumption that a "great" writer must be male. Margaret Oliphant and Anne Thackeray Ritchie are mentioned in a list with Meredith, Blackmore, Black, Payn, etc., as giving "hope for future" of the novel (34), and *Silas Marner* is cited as "the most *perfect* of English novels" (29), but that very emphasis would indicate the "*finesse* of detail" which is being valued. Besant regrets the denial to English novelists of national honors (which Hawthorne must do without in any case), but the distinctions which are mentioned—a peerage, a place in an academy— are not normally tendered to women. Indeed, women do not figure as subjects at all in Besant's essay on fiction. While he can expatiate on the work of Payn, Reade, Jeffries, and Kingsley, he "always thought, for instance,

> that the figure of Daniel Deronda, whose portrait, blurred and uncertain as it is, has been drawn with the most amazing care and with endless touches and retouches, must have become at last to

George Eliot a kind of awful veiled spectre, always in her brain,
always seeming about to reveal his true features and his mind, but
never doing it, so that to the end she never clearly perceived what
manner of man he was, nor what was his real character. (21)

A woman never serves as a competent subject in Besant's discourse on
writers, although women are frequently *objects*, as in his anecdote about
"a girl who brought [a writer] her first effort for advice and criticism,"
but "had not the least idea that there was such a thing as style" (26).
Again, he constructs an analogy between those who dismiss the element of "story" and women "who put on the newest and most prepos-
terous fashions gravely, and look upon each other without either
laughing or hiding their faces for shame" (28). The great writer's "experience," for Besant, must be British and male; in an 1887 essay, Besant
was to write: "The pens I hear . . . are the pens of girls trying to write
stories and burning to write novels." [15] In these ways, while Besant's
essay on the art of fiction makes assertions of literary value throughout—"incomparable tale," "great novel," "highest art," "highest order,"
"great Masters"—the "reason" of his judgments is to be found in their
apparent incoherences or incompletenesses. These judgments allude
to ideologies of literary value which, with the show of method, the professional pride, and the class complacency, make the whole essay
"reasonable." In this structure of ideological assumptions, rather than
in his provocation of Henry James or his contributions elsewhere to
English life, resides the historical significance of "Walter Besant" which
I want to assert in my analysis of *All Sorts and Conditions of Men*.

In 1897 Walter Besant wrote, in a "Preface to a New Edition" of
All Sorts and Conditions of Men, that the novelist

looks abroad, he observes, he receives, he reflects. That novelist
becomes most popular who is best able to catch and to represent the
ideas of the day, the forces acting on the present. I think that this
story did so present the ideas of the day. [16]

While his self-satisfaction might be justified—since its serialization in
Belgravia in 1882, *All Sorts and Conditions of Men* had sold 1,500 copies
as a three-decker, 20,000 at 3s. 6d., and 25,000 at 2s., [17] and by 1897
the People's Palace had been built in the Mile End Road—his analysis
of his success as a popular novelist is, as we shall see, not very acute.

Besant's story indeed presented some "ideas of the day," but more significant, again, were those which he took for granted. Besant, as self-
proclaimed "profound optimist," thought that "all history cries aloud
and proclaims with trumpet-note the fact that the meaning of the world
is the ordained advance of humanity" (vii), and the *Times* reviewer of
the serial *All Sorts and Conditions of Men* discerned a "vein of wild
originality" in the novel's portrayal of "a social Utopia, where unlimited
wealth uniting with wisdom and virtue accomplishes miracles by
patience and tact." [18] Other reviewers were less tolerant of the fanciful
element in the novel (which the *Fortnightly* called in 1883 "a ridiculous
book"): "it is not a pleasant sight," Henry Norman wrote,

> to see Mr Besant frisking about in the solemn fields of political
> economy. . . . Not even Mr Besant's charming story-telling and warm
> human sympathies can cover up such impracticable and unwise
> teachings as these. [19]

The *Nation*, from the United States, felt that the story was weakened
by "the unnecessary amount of philanthropy which is infused into
it." [20] These contemporary reviewers clearly did not look abroad and
observe the same ordained advance of humanity as Walter Besant. And
yet *All Sorts and Conditions of Men* was a very successful novel, suggesting
that the relation of Besant's "frisky" philanthropy to the solemn fields
of political economy is itself part of the ideological structure of the
novel, the social action he teaches taking its meaning only in the
simultaneous possibility of its opposite, sociopolitical stasis, of its direct
contradiction, political lethargy, and even in the possibility, or threat,
of political and social revolution. [21]

The story of *All Sorts and Conditions of Men* is quite simple. In 1881
("last year"), Angela Messenger, a graduate of Newnham College, Cambridge, and heiress to a large brewery in the East End of London, decides
to live in Stepney under an assumed name, to set up a model cooperative
workplace for seamstresses, and to do other beneficent works. At about
the same time, Harry Goslett, raised and educated as a gentleman by
his dead father's military commander, is told of his East End origins
and decides to acquaint himself with his dead father's world by working as a cabinetmaker in Stepney. Angela and Harry meet in their
boardinghouse in Stepney Green, and the novel unfolds the progress
of their life, their shared benevolent activities, and the revelation of

their true identities. Harry must discover the true circumstances of his having become the ward of Lord Jocelyn, which discovery establishes his fortune. But *All Sorts and Conditions of Men* has "a remarkably disintegrated structure,"[22] and these two strands of plot are entwined with the stories of their somewhat down-and-out fellow boarders: a professional conjurer, a junior clerk in the Messenger brewery, a carver of ships' figureheads, an Australian who has discovered "the primitive Alphabet and the Universal Language,"[23] and an elderly American couple who, despite their native republicanism, hope to establish their noble lineage and to claim an estate in Britain. With Harry's assistance, Angela (Messenger) Kennedy makes a success of her dressmaker's cooperative, and together they go on to found a "Palace of Delight," a large community center where the East Enders may enjoy reading, music, dancing, and other liberal pursuits. At the opening of the Palace, Angela reveals her identity to the world, and she and Harry are married. Fred W. Boege says of all of Besant and Rice's novels: "the love stories with few exceptions are typically Victorian, the figures unreal, the passionate side of love supplanted by unctious [*sic*] cadences about the influence of a good woman,"[24] and *All Sorts and Conditions of Men* fits this pattern. It mixes genres and modes—realist novel, romance, parody, exhortation—and everywhere displays Besant's amiable humor. He subtitled *All Sorts and Conditions of Men* "An Impossible Story," although, he said in his 1882 preface, "I have never been able to understand why it is impossible" (viii). The question of the "possibility" of its story is determined by the conditions of possibility of its text, which I now want to examine.

Of the two plots, Harry Goslett's is simpler and more conventional. In Stepney he learns that there is a mystery surrounding his adoption by Lord Jocelyn. He suspects villainy and finally discovers a cache of papers (the "discovered manuscript topos")[25] which unmasks the villain, thereby recovering his inheritance. Here the reader merely waits until Harry obtains his just deserts. Angela Messenger's story, on the other hand, while the conventional tale of a middle-class woman ("a princess disguised as a milkmaid" [245]) who chooses to devote her life and wealth to the poor, is complicated by conflicting genre expectations, with the romance elements—"what can rich people have more than society, lights, music, singing and dancing?" (142)—constantly coming up against Besant's gestures toward social realism in his specifics of locale and his insistence that all this happened "last year," among "the warm days of last September" (112). He is very specific about the novel's setting:

> There lies on the west and south-west of Stepney Green a triangular district, consisting of an irregular four-sided figure—what Euclid beautifully calls a trapezium—formed by the Whitechapel Road, the Commercial Road, Stepney Green and High Street, or Jamaica Street, or Jubilee Street, whichever you please to call your frontier. This favoured spot exhibits in perfection all the leading features which characterise the great Joyless City. It is, in fact, the heart of the East End. Its streets are mean and without individuality or beauty; at no season and under no conditions can they ever be picturesque; one can tell, without inquiring, that the lives led in those houses are all after the same model, and that the inhabitants have no pleasures. Everything that goes to make a city, except the means of amusement, is to be found here. (132)

This is but one of many passages in which Besant proudly shows his familiarity with East End geography, inviting our assent to the novel's realism. Charles Booth's investigators, a decade later, were to insist that 26.2 percent of the lives led in the houses of the northeast segment of Besant's trapezium were "in poverty," but then Booth's assistants had inquired, while Besant could tell without inquiring that the lives led in those houses were all after "the same model," joyless, lacking gardens, avenues, theaters, art galleries, libraries.[26] I shall return to the narrator's position in this passage, but I want to continue with the novel's treatment of sorts and conditions.

There were particular sorts, or groups, in the East End of London in the 1880s which Besant patronizes or dismisses in his novel: not only political radicals,[27] but also "Seventh Day Independents" and the Salvation Army. It is the tone, again, of his disagreement which is significant. Rebekah Hermitage, the Independent, "never give[s] way in the matter of truth" (71). He comments sarcastically: "What a splendid, what a magnificent field of glory—call it not vain-glory!—does this conviction present to the humble believer!" (248). Harry's cousin, Captain Tom Coppin of the Salvation Army, "a man of the people, self-taught, profoundly ignorant as to the many problems of life and their many solutions" (218–19), is the butt of a similar easy irony. When he preaches at Angela's workrooms, "this place which offered pleasure instead of repentance as a method of improving life" (216), he resorts to "a kind of rhetorical trick which often proves effective," and Angela must intervene because "his creed was narrow, his truths only half-truths, his doctrine commonplace, his language in bad taste, his manner vulgar" (288, 287). In his *Autobiography*, Besant was to write, "Christianity seems to me a perfectly simple religion,"[28] blandly dismissing many problems, if not many solutions. But while he may have often praised the work of the religious agencies in his later writings,[29] *All Sorts and Conditions of Men* constructs a position from which false prophets, religious and secular alike, may be easily dismissed.

This, too, is a kind of rhetorical trick, which shows itself most clearly in the kind of statement of social faith that Henry Goslett makes. "All sorts and conditions of men are pretty much alike," Harry says, rejecting a class analysis ("in the lump") of workingmen (136). That particular group, the working class in the lump, is the group whose existence the novel most insistently denies. "Who is 'us'?" an old Chartist asks (238), and early on, Lord Jocelyn remarks to Harry: "there are indeed—at least, I suppose so—all sorts and conditions of men. But to me, and to men brought up like you and me, I do not understand how there can be any but one sort and one condition" (14). Harry agrees, and so does the narrator. Angela, in an exchange with Lord Jocelyn, claims that "women of all ranks, like men, are the same" (172). The novel reconciles "all sorts" with "one sort" by emphasizing human diversity and individuality, as with Angela's working girls: a common type, but "so common, alas! that we are apt to forget the individuality of each, her personal hopes, and her infinite possibilities" (94). "Each life," says Harry, "is individual, and has its own separate interests" (48).

That this conclusion is so banal is precisely its significance: it is merely a restatement of bourgeois individualism as a universalizing and harmlessly unifying principle for the England of the 1880s. For while Besant's novel may contrast its "all sorts" to *some* sorts (such as sects and such social groupings), and even to *no* sorts (common types), it cannot consider or comprehend those structured, diverse sorts, like determinate classes, which were being considered elsewhere in the 1880s. The banality of Besant's ideological position signals its defensiveness, both that it *is* defensive and what it defends. In this it connects with some of the other positions I have mentioned, the religious chauvinism and, particularly, the narrative point of view. "One can tell, without inquiring, that the lives led in those houses are all after the same model"—"at least I suppose so," Lord Jocelyn might have added. Besant's idea of human life, for all his emphases on diversity, is narrowly English middle class. The rest of the world exists in the novel as places— Australia, America—to come from, just as the religious and political sects do not need to be taken seriously. Class differences are dealt with in the same genial way—"There is, indeed, so little difference between the rich and the poor; can even Hyde Park in the season go beyond the flower and the cigar?" (112). Significantly, Angela, the heiress (who apparently has complete access to her wealth), "slightly reddens at men-tion of the money" (153–54) and "colours" when she is asked, "who is going to pay for all this?" (80). Her liberal diffidence, established in contrast to Lord Jocelyn's liberal complacency and Harry Goslett's benevolent energy, gives the novel its peculiar limping dynamic— peculiar because it so resolutely refuses to contemplate the revolutionary threat, and limping because that yet lurks as an unspoken contrary/ contradiction.

All Sorts and Conditions of Men was serialized from January to December 1882, in *Belgravia*, which was Chatto and Windus' "clone" of Smith, Elder's *Cornhill*: a shilling monthly literary review edited by the popular novelist M. E. Braddon. Like *Temple Bar*, founded by Mrs. Braddon's husband, John Maxwell, *Belgravia* was produced "for the com-fortable, literate, but ill-educated middle-class which read magazines for pure entertainment and easy instruction."[30] Chatto and Windus then published *All Sorts and Conditions of Men* in three volumes in October 1882, just before it ended its run as a serial, and brought out the 3s. 6d. edition in January 1884 and the 2s. "railway" edition in May 1884—only in 1900 did they publish it in a 6d. paper-cover edition. Simon Eliot not only provides this information in his long and valuable study of the novel, but also suggests ways of reading the publishing history of *All Sorts and Conditions of Men* and, further, some initial conclusions. I shall incorporate his work into my own analysis of the entrepreneurial production of that commodity-text. Eliot, for exam-ple, analyzes Chatto and Windus' advertising practice around the novel, contrasting it to their usual practice:

> From January to August 1882 each monthly part of *All Sorts and Conditions of Men* was advertised at least once in the *Athenaeum*, and on no less than five of these eight occasions the Chatto and Windus advertisement also included notices of Besant and Rice novels in their 3s6d and 2s forms. Thus the firm's advertising policy,

as far as Besant and Rice were concerned, shows a marked difference in the first six months of 1882 from what it had been in previous years.[31]

Eliot notes other details—how frequently the names of Besant and Rice appear in the ads, and where they are positioned—and later he analyzes the size of the reprintings of the novel and the speed with which these occur compared with usual practices, as indications of Chatto and Windus' perception of popularity and demand. The point is that here, as in their advertising *All Sorts and Conditions of Men*, Chatto and Windus change their practice: "Clearly, Besant is beginning to look like a bestseller to his publishers." But Eliot's account of the novel's promotion goes well beyond the details of print runs; he speculates on the reasons for Chatto's initially attributing in their ads *All Sorts and Conditions of Men* to both Besant and Rice, although Rice, dying of cancer, had no part in its production. He considers various personal reasons and concludes: "whatever other reasons lay behind this promise of yet another Besant and Rice novel, it certainly made good business sense. It offered a product which was well-known and, within its limitations, reliable and competent." Eliot frequently alludes to aspects of "reassuring familiarity," from the first advertisement to the conventionality and complacency of the novel itself,[32] and I would like to comment further on these matters, working from an initial generalization.

I would suggest that the conditions of production of *All Sorts and Conditions of Men*, as Simon Eliot explains them, exemplify the practice of an entrepreneurial publisher in negotiating and exploring the range of the familiar for a particular audience. At first, from December 1881, the "familiar" is Besant's association with James Rice and their jointly authored novels, and *All Sorts and Conditions of Men* is advertised as from their partnership. But "at least by October 1882, *All Sorts and Conditions of Men* is admitted to be by one author." By now, and as the three-volume edition is about to appear, nine installments have appeared in *Belgravia*, and it is clear to his readers that Besant's novel is the familiar article. But by now, as well, "the familiar" can be seen to be deeply rooted in this particular text. Simon Eliot discusses a theme of Besant's presentment of Harry's activities in the East End, the theme of "generating a proper discontent rather than a conventional one": "In Harry's view, an unthinkingly conventional attitude to politics has led to a combination of stoicism and complacency." But Eliot goes on,

calling *All Sorts and Conditions of Men* "essentially a rhetorical novel,"
to ask rightly:

> what can one say for an argument that bases itself upon the compla-
> cent assumption that, in the 1880s, there was nothing very much
> wrong economically with the East End and East Enders?[33]

Fred Boege pointed out a characteristic setting, almost a trademark,
of Besant's later novels, "a benign picture of a world designed solely
for the welfare and joy of its human inhabitants,"[34] and Edith Sichel
suggested in *Murray's Magazine* in 1888 that Besant always seems
to be writing "from out the midst of a cozy haze of blue tobacco
smoke."[35] Harry's unconventionality is, in fact, conveniently conventional and complacent, and, to Besant's audience, reassuringly familiar.
There seemed to be in this period "an almost simple relation between
sentimental optimism and popular acclaim,"[36] and *All Sorts and Conditions of Men* can be seen as an ideological structure for producing a
comfortable complacency about the East End, a "reasonable" solution
of its problems. The preconstructed discourse of this text, so to speak,
its "ordinarinesses," intersects with a transverse discourse, the "wild-
ness" of whose originality (in the *Times*'s phrase) incapacitates it. The
openhandedness of the heiress, the easy success of her cooperative
workshop cum summer camp, the promise of her "Palace of Delight"
(so little radical that a Peoples' Palace was actually built), all of these
represent a "reasonable," because "wild," originality, a discourse which
"transverses" the utterly conventional, preconstructed discourse at a
very acute angle. The very simplicity of Besant's argumentative structures, the fact "that he is often able to expose a current platitude or
conventional way of thinking by insisting on the truth of its opposite,"
or by turning "small-scale truths" into "large, incredible generalizations,"[37] is the simplicity of one who either does not need to inquire
or trusts to "reason." And these are obviously familiar habits of mind,
presenting no challenges to the *Belgravia*'s readers or to Mudie's sub-
scribers. They explore, for the entrepreneurial Chatto and Windus, the
range of the familiar for a middle-class audience and represent the structure of a best-selling text, the aim of the enterprising publisher.

2. Henry James's "The Art of Fiction" was not presented as a lecture: rather it was written in the "ferment" (as Leon Edel put it) produced by his month in Paris in the winter of 1884, when he visited

Daudet, Zola, and Edmond de Goncourt. It first appeared in *Longman's Magazine*, in September 1884, in response to Besant's pamphlet. *Longman's* would seem an unlikely place for Henry James to publish anything; indeed, he was to publish only one other piece in *Longman's* in his lifetime, "The Pupil" in 1891, and then only after it had been unexpectedly rejected by the *Atlantic* and he had consulted a literary agent.[38] *Longman's* was an odd place because, unlike the *Atlantic*, which maintained "a high character and a reputation for conservatism,"[39] *Longman's* was a 6d. monthly, started in 1882, representing "an early venture in the field of mass marketing," a venture which was somewhat miscalculated, as Walter Houghton writes, because "Longman's 'bold step' amounted to generously subsidizing a middle-class appetite for pleasant fiction and agreeably informative articles." Although C. J. Longman edited the magazine himself, his chief literary advisor was his close friend Andrew Lang, whose monthly department, "At the Sign of the Ship," "made him a household word in middle-class, middle-brow parlors." Lang was also the "clever writer" who had contributed anonymously an article[40] to the *Pall Mall Gazette* commenting on Besant's original lecture in which, because of his "strong prejudice against psychological and realistic novels,"[41] he had disparaged "certain tales in which 'Bostonian nymphs' appear to have 'rejected English dukes for psychological reasons.' "[42] There appear to be no records surviving of the editorial affairs of *Longman's Magazine* at this time, but Henry James, who was later to describe Lang to R. L. Stevenson as using "his beautiful thin facility to write everything down to the lowest level of Philistine twaddle—the view of the old lady round the corner or the clever person at the dinner party,"[43] clearly employs its pages to make his case indirectly against Lang, while addressing Besant directly. But by publishing his essay in *Longman's*, James also was making his case before Lang's "popular" audience, with a middle-class appetite and taste ("that of the library subscriber") for "agreeably informative articles," which perhaps in part determined the ironic "modesty and the tentativeness" of his remarks on Besant, "one of the mildest (and most devastating) reproofs in literary history."[44]

In the main, James reproves Besant by rearranging and redefining the terms of his discourse. Whereas Besant was presenting his attempt at a *science* of fiction, James begins by asserting that although in the past there was only "a comfortable, good-humoured feeling abroad that a novel is a novel, as a pudding is a pudding, and that this was the end of it" (54), now we are able to have a *theory* of the novel. The novel, for James, is no longer simply "out there," to be naively, and "scientifically," examined for its "rules" and "laws." The novel is now "*discutable*": we may now see, not mere pudding, but the different incompletenesses in the form of the novels, say, of Dickens and Thackeray (54). His distinction between "pudding" and "form" is precisely the distinction we might make between empirical and theoretical knowledge, and James proceeds to enforce that distinction throughout his essay. Besant insisted that fiction is one of the *fine* arts—in fact he demanded "not only that it shall be reputed artistic, but that it shall be reputed very artistic indeed." James rubs his eyes that this proposition should be thought a novelty (58), just as he objects to Besant's "rather unguarded talk" about the novelist's practice of "selection." James insists that the selection that matters must have a theoretical component, not be merely a rearrangement: "Art is essentially selection, but it is a selection whose main care is to be typical, to be inclusive" (75–76). The typical is also to be distinguished from what, at an earlier moment in his essay, James called "certain traditions on the subject, applied *a priori*" (61). In both places in the essay James's discussion immediately moves to the issue of artistic "freedom": art "lives on exercise, and the very meaning of exercise is freedom" (62), and, later, a "seriously artistic attempt" produces "an immense increase—a kind of revelation—of freedom" (76). "There is no limit," James says, "to what [the novelist] may attempt as an executant—no limit to his possible experiments, efforts, discoveries, successes" (63), a position intended to counter the ordinary, middle-class complacency of Besant's lecture. And in both places in his essay the mention of freedom leads immediately to a discussion of the artist's temperament: "a novel is . . . a direct impression of life" (62), since the province of art is "all experience" (76). We are moved very quickly, as Taylor Stoehr points out, "from the representing of 'life' to the reporting of 'experience' to the recording of 'impressions.'"[45] This triad, then, *selection* (as the search for the "typical"), the necessary *freedom* it entails, and *experience* (as a *direct impression* of life), articulates James's position on artistic production, his theoretical rebuttal of Besant's "science" of fiction in "The Art of Fiction."

"If experience consists of impressions, it may be said that impressions *are* experience" (67);

> [Experience] is an immense sensibility, a kind of huge spider-web, of
> the finest silken threads, suspended in the chamber of consciousness
> and catching every air-borne particle in its tissue. It is the very
> atmosphere of the mind. (65–66)

Nothing could be further removed than this from Besant's positivist,
"scientific" preoccupation with, say, the limited experience of a young
lady brought up in a quiet country village. Experience is sensibility,
and so, James says, "the young lady has only to be a damsel upon whom
nothing is lost" (66). In contrast to Besant's example, Charles Reade's
description of France in the fewest possible words—"by the mere action
of the piece and the dialogue we are compelled to see the scenery"—
James tells of the impression "a woman of genius," Anne Thackeray
Ritchie, was able to give of the nature and way of life of French Protestant youth from having once glimpsed a French Protestant family at
a meal:

> The glimpse made a picture; it lasted only a moment, but that
> moment was experience. She had got her direct personal impression,
> and she evolved her type. (66)

Again, James has shifted the terrain of Besant's discussion, from the
vague, empiricist comment on Reade's few words and the "action of
the piece," to Ritchie's experience, as sensibility, from which she produces a "reality." Given an inch, she took an ell, and so, James repeats,
"I should certainly say to a novice . . . : 'Try to be one of the people
on whom nothing is lost' " (67). For Henry James, "the deepest quality
of a work of art will always be the quality of the mind of the producer"
(83). A fine intelligence entails "the power to guess the unseen from
the seen, to trace the implication of things," and constitutes "experience" for James (67).

These would seem to be the issues, as well, for James in *The Princess
Casamassima* (1886). Its "prime idea," he was to write in the preface
to the New York edition (1909) of the novel, was "unmistakeably the
ripe round fruit of perambulation," that is, the "attentive exploration
of London," but that exploration transformed by "sensibility." In 1909
James recalled "the assault directly made by the great city upon an
imagination quick to react,"[46] and the novel explores just that mode
of experience, "the sentient faculty of a youth on whom nothing was

lost" (164). James's narrator never presents a description of London equivalent to that of Besant's "trapezium" in Stepney; rather, London is "experienced" by the characters in ways which measure their sensibilities.

The Princess Casamassima presents as an issue "knowing" the world and its inhabitants, having that sensibility on which nothing is lost since it turns "experience" into knowledge. In his 1909 preface, James distinguishes his own experience from Hyacinth's, since for James himself all the doors in London were opened to the "freedom and ease, knowledge and power, money, opportunity, and satiety," of which "the swarming facts" of London spoke (34). Hyacinth's "natural and immediate London," on the other hand, was the experience of "the meaner conditions, the lower manners and types, the general sordid struggle, the weight of the burden of labor, the ignorance, the misery and the vice" (35). James's artistic problem in The Princess Casamassima, as he remembered it in 1906, had been that "the agents in any drama, are interesting only in proportion as they feel their respective situations":

> it is those . . . who "get most" out of all that happens to them and who in so doing enable us, as readers of their record, as participators by a fond attention, also to get most. (35)

Theoretically at least (and twenty years after The Princess Casamassima was published), Henry James rejected the easy epistemological complacencies of a Walter Besant. If the generic conventions of the working-class novel are "the socially conscious aristocrat, typically female, who goes to work in the slums; the lower-class stiff who, through luck and initiative, wins a place (often through marriage) in the middle class—neither of whom finally threatens the existing class structure in any fundamental way," then The Princess Casamassima leans as heavily on these "precedents"[47] as does All Sorts and Conditions of Men. But a comparison of the two novels makes vivid the essential difference in their use of the genre. While Besant assumes full knowledge, his own and his characters', of the "slums" of Stepney, and complacently maneuvers his upper-class female and lower-class stiff around his "trapezium," James sets as his central theme Hyacinth's coming to know his setting (or his settings, since he comes to "know" not only the East End, but "Medley," the Princess's rented country estate, and, most important, Paris and Venice). And Hyacinth comes to know these not as *locale*, but as the type (or as James might also say, the "note" [114])[48] of a place. It is the consequences, or indeed the overdeterminations, of this different idea of knowledge that I now want to explore.

Hyacinth's capacity for this sort of knowledge is first indicated by his ironical propensity—"even at the age of ten Hyacinth Robinson was ironical" (61). His first visit to the invalid Rose Muniment is an early exercise in social judgment. The narrator says, "she was not a common woman," and hastens to add that "Hyacinth did not define her in this manner to himself" (137); a little later we are told: "After Hyacinth knew more of the world he remembered this tone [or 'note'] of Muniment's sister" (137). When Lady Aurora mentions "the upper class, the people that have got all the things," Hyacinth corrects her: " 'We don't call them the people' . . . , reflecting the next instant that his remark was a little primitive" (140).[49] Again, although he at first thinks that Paul Muniment sees him as a potential comrade in "a subterranean crusade against the existing order of things," it later comes over him that the "real use" he had been put to was simply to entertain Muniment's sister (152). Hyacinth thus also gradually learns to "know" his social surroundings. The story of his personal relationship to the Princess and to Muniment reaches its climax, "inexpressibly representative to him" (and twice commented on), when, standing with the Prince, he sees Muniment, after pausing outside, reenter her house with the Princess (520, 535, 536). The novel thus minutely traces (as it defines ever more clearly) the growth of Hyacinth's ability to "feel" his "situation" (35), which includes his personal relations to a locale, to other characters, to the *class* situation and, less clearly, to the subterranean crusade, the revolutionary movement, which has ensnared him. We might map the ideological terrain which the novel here explores as, again, a "square" or "rectangle," plotted on the manifest level by the "ignorance"/"knowledge" binary, and by their contraries/contradictories in this novel, "envy" or, tellingly, "taste." Hyacinth, for example, comes to know Millicent Henning as a type, "magnificently plebeian, in the sense that implied a kind of loud recklessness of danger and the qualities that shine forth in a row" (160), and his "knowledge" of class generally is also progressively conditioned by this set of relations, as when the "familiar phenomena" of "the great, roaring indifferent world of London" become "symbolic, insolent, defiant" (164). The novel contrasts Hyacinth's growth in knowledge to, say, Lady Aurora's: "Are we on the eve of great changes, or are we not?" (200), and to the patronizing curiosity, the want of fine tact, of Captain Sholto toward the working class:

> The Captain requested information as to the position in life, the avocations and habits, of the other lodgers, the rent they paid, their relations with each other, both in and out of the family. "Now, would there be a good deal of close packing, do you suppose, and any perceptible want of—a—sobriety?" (228)

This range of examples provides Hyacinth with "the best opportunities for choosing between the beauty of the original and the beauty of the conventional" (524). He moves, for example, from perceiving merely the peculiarity of Lady Aurora's pronunciation of the letter *r* (134) to his recognition that "her ladyship was an original, and an original with force" (222), just as he moves from his headstrong commitment at the "Sun and Moon," vowing to do "anything that will do any good; anything, anything—I don't care a rap" (294), to his doleful change of heart: "He saw the immeasurable misery of the people, and yet he saw all that had been, as it were, rescued and redeemed from it: the treasures, the felicities, the splendours, the successes of the world" (445). For "the central opposition" for Hyacinth, as John Goode says, "is between art and change."[50] He is portrayed from his early days as exhibiting toward the rich no "morbid vanity" or "personal jealousy that could not be intelligent"; "his personal discomfort was the result of an exquisite admiration for what he had missed" (165). His letter to the Princess from Venice (after his experience of Paris, and of Medley) speaks of his horror of a "grudging attitude," "that kind of invidious jealousy which is at the bottom of the idea of a redistribution" (397), and upon his return to London he sees vividly "the social jealousy lying at the bottom of the desire for a fresh deal [of the social pack]" (404, 403):

> Everywhere, everywhere, he saw the ulcer of envy—the passion of a party which hung together for the purpose of despoiling another to its advantage. (405)

As political analysis of working-class discontent in 1879–82,[51] this would be no more respectable than Walter Besant's, but it takes its meaning only within the ideological field of the text of *The Princess Casamassima*. For while Hyacinth perceives that he has been presented, in the Princess and Millicent, with opportunities for choosing between the beauty of the original and the beauty of the conventional, the novel as a whole contemplates this "choice" within a field which also includes "eternal" beauty (as of Venice) and beauty or value resulting from class struggle (Yeats's "terrible beauty"). Hyacinth's "choice," which, as ideology, cannot know these multiple determinations, may thus be seen as entirely contradictory and contrary, as a free, detached exercise of what is called "taste."

The ideology of "taste" dominates the latter part of *The Princess Casamassima*. Hyacinth Robinson's apprenticeship as a bookbinder was an early education of his sensibility, training him in "the finest discriminations" (157). His encounter with the Princess continues this particular branch of his education, as he learns at Medley "that the knowledge of luxury and the extension of one's sensations beget a taste for still newer pleasures" (339). His visit to Paris gives his sensations and knowledge an Arnoldian bias:

> he felt as if hitherto he had lived in a dusky, frowsy, Philistine world, in which the taste was the taste of Little Peddlington and the ideal of beautiful arrangement had never had an influence. (383)

And in Paris his commitment to overthrowing the social order is lost and is replaced by the sense of the "wonderful, precious things" which the social order has produced, of "the brilliant, impressive fabric it had raised" (382–83). Then, in Venice, this particular aestheticization of experience becomes his habitual practice; he writes to the Princess of how he casts his genial (this time almost Ruskinian) eye on the Venetian women, "dressed in thin, cheap cotton gowns, whose limp folds make the same delightful line that everything else in Italy makes":

> The Venetian girl-face is wonderfully sweet and the effect is charming when its pale, sad oval (they all look underfed) is framed in the old faded shawl. (394)

Hyacinth's developed taste, then, is neither for the beauty of the original nor for the beauties of the conventional, but is rather a more familiar, high-Victorian, cultured taste, and when he returns to London he finds that he loathes the people among whom he works: "he knew and hated every article they wore" (403). Hyacinth feels himself able now to judge the social significance of the Princess's move to Madeira Crescent: "not squalid" but "mean and meagre and fourth-rate." He decides that with her move the Princess's commitment to the "poor" plainly entails making herself suffer "the anguish of exasperated taste." Madeira Crescent had in the highest degree

> that paltry, parochial air, that absence of style and elevation, which is the stamp of whole districts of London and which Hyacinth had already more than once mentally compared with the high-piled, important look of the Parisian perspective. (417, 421)

That comparison significantly distinguishes Hyacinth from the Princess. Whereas she would have considered it the worst taste to bring to her work among the people "a pretension of greater delicacy and finer manners" (248), and now cannot tell the difference, she says, between bad bookbinding and good (475), Hyacinth Robinson has become less impressed by the misery of the poor than by "their brutal insensibility, a grossness impervious to the taste of better things or to any desire for them" (477). As he wrote to the Princess from Venice, "the splendid accumulations of the happier few, to which, doubtless, the miserable many have also in their degree contributed . . . seem to me inestimably precious and beautiful" (396). To this has come "a sensibility on which nothing is lost"; as John Goode says, "History becomes a matter of curios."[52] What finally prevents Hyacinth from fulfilling his assassin's vow, and drives him to suicide, is the development of his exquisite taste. His position in the novel's field of possibilities, in contrast or contradiction to those of originary beauty, conventional beauty, and revolutionary beauty, is one of isolated "free" choice, dictated by an achieved good taste. The social isolation of this position betrays itself in a peculiar narrative uncertainty in the text of *The Princess Casamassima*.

   The Princess Casamassima was serialized in the *Atlantic Monthly* from September 1885 to October 1886, and on 22 October 1886, just as it ended its serial run, Macmillan published the three-volume edition for the British market. Macmillan also printed, in October 1886, a one-volume edition for both the British and American markets, releasing the American issue in November, but holding the 6s. English issue until August 1887,[53] thereby giving Mudie's a ten-month's monopoly with the three-decker. This production schedule protected James's copyright in both countries,[54] and it contrasts with the "indecent haste," the mere three-month interval that Chatto and Windus allowed between the three-volume *All Sorts and Conditions of Men* and its 3s. 6d. reprint. But Chatto was an entrepreneurial publisher—the price of its reprint "Piccadilly Library" was lowered from 6s. in the 1870s to 3s. 6d. in the 1880s[55]—and Macmillan was not. Macmillan's catalogues, Charles Morgan wrote, "year by year, have a consistency of their own—or the kind of related inconsistency that goes to the making of an individual character," and it is this kind of consistency which turns a "catalogue" into a "list": "Endurance is the aim; the deliberately topical, unless there is a promise of endurance in it, is little sought after."[56] In 1886, besides *The Princess Casamassima*, Macmillan pursued this aim with a list including their usual books of sermons, a reprint of selected chapters of Thomas Arnold's history of Rome (1838–43), *The Early Letters of Thomas Carlyle* in two volumes, a facsimile of the original MS of *Alice's Adventures Under Ground*, Sir John Lubbock's *Flowers, Fruits and Leaves* in their "Nature Series," as well as three new volumes in their "Elementary Classics" series, two in their "Classical Series" and thirty-four new volumes in "Macmillan's Colonial Library," "for circulation only in India and the Colonies."[57] Thus, even had James's prediction to his brother William been correct, that "The *Princess* will, I trust, appear more 'popular'" than his previous novels,[58] Macmillan's publishing practice would have prevented exploiting this popularity entrepreneurially. Macmillan's first and only printing of the three-volume *Princess Casamassima* consisted of 750 copies; the first edition of *All Sorts and Conditions of Men* had been 1,500, 750 to 1,500 sets being the normal size for Chatto's first editions. And whereas Chatto's 3s. 6d. one-volume reprint of Besant's novel was for 6,000 copies (with two further impressions, 3,000 copies each, within eight months), Macmillan reprinted their one-volume *Princess Casamassima* in an edition of 3,000 copies for both the domestic and American markets. The yellow-back edition of *All Sorts and Conditions of Men* in 1884 consisted of 8,000 volumes, "a large but not exceptionally large print run"; in 1888 Macmillan issued a yellow-back of James's novel in two printings of 2,000 copies each.[59] Macmillan was clearly counting on *The Princess Casamassima*'s promise of endurance to make it "a Macmillan book."[60]

The *Bibliography of Henry James* asserts that there were only "minor revisions" between serial and book publication,[61] but this appears to be incorrect. Whereas Macmillan's three volumes, and, I presume, every subsequent edition, divides the novel into *six* "Books," the *Atlantic Monthly* serial is divided into *five*.[62] This major formal revision indicates the narrative uncertainty I have referred to, and which James recorded in his notebook in August 1885:

> It is absolutely necessary that at this point I should make the future evolution of the *Princess Casamassima* more clear to myself. I have never yet become engaged in a novel in which, after I had begun to write and send off my MS., the details had remained so vague.[63]

The difference in the two editions is significant because, like the chapter divisions but unlike the three volumes, it is a matter not of format but of form. In the five-book serial in the *Atlantic*, the third book begins at Medley, the Princess's countryhouse, three months after Hyacinth's going to meet with Hoffendahl and taking his assassin's vow; it encompasses Miss Pynsent's death, Hyacinth's trips to Paris and Venice and his change of heart, his return to London, and the Princess's increasing revolutionary involvement, marked by her move to Madeira Crescent. Book 4, then, begins with Hyacinth's visits, first to Madeira Crescent and then to Lady Aurora in Belgrave Square, and ends with the appearance of Schinkel, who bears Hoffendahl's assignment to Hyacinth. The book division here foregrounds two large movements in the midst of James's narrative: the first recounts the history, after his vow, of Hyacinth's growing appreciation of the glories of Western civilization and his accompanying gradual disavowal; the second recounts his alienation from the Princess and the intrusion of Paul Muniment—the sight of the Princess's door closing on Muniment's back effectively ends the action of book 4 in the serial. Thus the central action of the novel is shaped in the *Atlantic* serial into an account of the Hyacinth/Princess/Muniment revolutionary triangle, a pavane of personal and political relations, changing as revolutionary ardor wanes and waxes. Moreover, the movement in five books, with its focus on Hyacinth, implies that this is a tragic shape. But in the three-decker and after (the familiar version), the identical sequence of events is shaped into six books, with the third and the fourth "acts" of Hyacinth's "tragedy" being redivided into three. Now Hyacinth is seen, not as the central figure of three in an interweaving of radical politics and human relationships, but rather as, more "realistically," the central figure moving from discrete event to discrete event as he, and we, await the consequences of his vow to Hoffendahl. The three-volume structure is thus more episodic, as James removes his underlining of the overarching rhythms of Hyacinth's story. The effect, I contend, is to disperse and mute the larger political rhythms, playing down their interplay (or "dance") with the personal and allowing more emphasis on what I have called the high-Victorian aesthetic. The "weave" of *The Princess Casamassima* has decidedly changed, rewriting in this way the ideology of the text.

There is no mention of this change in the Macmillan archives, nor in James's correspondence (nor, for that matter, in the criticism), and I can only speculate on its determinations. As Deborah Esch has pointed out in her recent essay on *The Princess Casamassima*:

> on closer consideration, the principal thematic categories—
> including the political—prove to be rent by a constitutive self-
> division within the language of their articulation with which a
> reading of the novel must come to terms.

The questions which *The Princess Casamassima* raises do not reside merely on "the thematic level of the text."[64] James had moved the novel from a monthly magazine with a central place in American literary culture to an English "list" publisher who was constrained by the three-volume/Mudie's structure and who almost a year later followed the three volumes by the usual "popular," one-volume printing. If the first, serial, text foregrounded, for a select American readership, the larger formal interplay of the political and personal themes, when publication was returned to London, this larger formal movement had to accommodate the more visible contemporaneity of its political story and the immediacy of its locale, while never, of course, disappearing. At the same time, the "list" publishing practices of James's English publisher prevented exploiting "the deliberately topical" or political, while favoring, perhaps, the social and aesthetic ideology of the particulars of Hyacinth's story. The thematic complexity of *The Princess Casamassima* is not simply antithetical to the easy complacencies of *All Sorts and Conditions of Men*, but also disrupts its text, which must try to reconcile its thematic contradictions with the material conditions of its transatlantic production.

3. It was not at all unusual that Robert Louis Stevenson's contribution to the "art of fiction debate," "A Humble Remonstrance," should

appear in *Longman's Magazine* (5 December 1884, 139–47). Stevenson had been a frequent contributer to *Longman's* since its first issue, in which "A Gossip on Romance" had appeared. More recently, *Prince Otto* had been serialized from April to December 1883, and the magazine had published "Old Mortality" in May 1884. The closeness of his connection to *Longman's Magazine* is, as we shall see, a first symptom of Stevenson's ideological difference from Henry James (as well as from Walter Besant), yet "A Humble Remonstrance" was the occasion of his first meeting James in 1885. For James wrote a quick and complimentary response to Stevenson's "suggestive and felicitous" published remarks, "justly felt and brilliantly said," and he claimed that "we agree, I think, much more than we disagree." "My pages, in *Longman,*" James wrote, "were simply a plea for liberty," implying Stevenson's general agreement at the same time as he implied the direction of Stevenson's reservations: "You will say that my 'liberty' is an obese divinity, requiring extra measures." [65] James's distinctions, and the admission that his "liberty" may not be very vigorous, can be the starting point for our discussion of Stevenson's "humble remonstrance" on the art of fiction.

While Stevenson was clearly as little impressed by Besant's paper as Henry James, like James he began his essay by commenting on Besant and, again like James, questioning Besant's terms. Not only does Besant use "poetry" as if it referred only to "verse," Stevenson noted, but his understanding of fiction is "both too ample and too scanty." Stevenson argues that both Besant and James are really talking about "the art of narrative." [66] While James explained his disagreement with Besant by saying that the novel exists not simply to *mirror* but to "compete with" life, Stevenson, stressing life's "majestic chords," "pageantry of life and colour" and "wealth of incident" (12:210), argues that fiction does not and cannot "compete" with life, but rather creates "a certain figmentary abstraction" (12:211), "a certain artificial series of impressions" (12:212). In this way he arrives at his first important conclusion:

> Life is monstrous, infinite, illogical, abrupt, and poignant; a work of art, in comparison, is neat, finite, self-contained, rational, flowing, and emasculate. (12:213)

The novel exists, says Stevenson, by its "designed and significant" difference from life (12:213). The root of the matter is that a novel is not "a transcript of life, to be judged by its exactitude; but a simplification of some side or point of life, to stand or fall by its significant simplicity" (12:222). This distinction originates in James's contention that the true novelist may work even from the "faintest hints of life," James's example being what Anne Thackeray Ritchie was able to do with merely a glimpse of a French Protestant family at supper, significant simplicity if ever there were. But Stevenson extends James's point, just as James went well beyond Besant's simple "man of experience," cutting loose from even a glimpse of "life" or "experience":

> it will be found true, I believe, in a majority of cases, that the artist writes with more gusto and effect of those things which he has only wished to do, than of those which he has done. Desire is a wonderful telescope, and Pisgah the best observatory. (12:215)

Distinguishing between novels of adventure, of character, and in the dramatic mode (12:214), Stevenson implies that the novel of adventure, his own *métier*, is truest to this conception, exhibiting the greatest gusto and desire. Not moral or intellectual interest, but danger and fear, the signs of desire, are appropriate to novels like *Treasure Island*, and the characters are portrayed "only so far as they realise the sense of danger and provoke the sympathy of fear" (12:216).

"A Gossip on Romance" appeared in the first issue of *Longman's Magazine*, in November 1882, and shared to some extent, we might assume, in C. J. Longman's aspirations as to audience and mode. There Stevenson first recalled how, as a boy, he read only for "some quality of the brute incident" (21:187). Out of that boyhood experience (generalizable because innocent) Stevenson developed his theory of romance. Again he distinguished "romance" from "drama": "Drama is the poetry of conduct, romance the poetry of circumstance. . . . Conduct is three parts of life, they say; but I think they put it too high" (21:188), and "they" is clearly the Matthew Arnold of *Literature and Dogma* and *God and the Bible*. Stevenson's nondramatic romance, the "poetry of circumstance," is thus free of Arnoldian morality—"there is a vast deal in life and letters which is not immoral, but simply nonmoral" (21:188). From the "fitness of events and places" it builds "the most lively, beautiful and buoyant tales." Romance arises, says Stevenson, from "the genius of the place and moment" (21:189); "The desire for knowledge, I had almost added the desire for meat, is not more deeply seated than this demand for fit and striking incident" (21:191–92). He then presents several formulations for what, I am arguing, he was to call "strength and honesty," "adventure," "romance," and in his "Humble Remonstrance," "significant simplicity." But here, in *Longman's* in 1882, "the great creative writer shows us the realisation and the apotheosis of the day-dreams of common men" (21:192). In populist phraseology like this Stevenson attempts to demonstrate what, a year later, he called "strength and honesty," or, more succinctly, *desire* (as in "the desire for meat").

My first comment on this progression, or succession of ideas, leading up to his "Humble Remonstrance" to James and Besant in 1884 is simply to note its use of convention, so unlike Besant's both in its easy *Longman's* sociability and in its invoking "simplicity," the "common," the "right" conventions. The "gusto" and "glamour" of romance, Stevenson claims, come upon him "like a surprise that I had expected" (21:199, 200), and I would argue that that paradox marks the contradiction that Stevenson maintains at the heart of his ideology of romance, conjoining the "surprise" of romance to the rationality of "expectation." This contradiction shows most often in Stevenson's appropriation of quantities of the feminine. He nowhere mentions a woman novelist in these three essays on the novel, nor, for that matter, does his 1887 essay "Books Which Have Influenced Me"—a discussion of about fifteen (but in 1887 implying "one hundred") authors—mention any woman author.[67] Moreover, his talk of "strength" and "gusto," "adventure" and "the day-dreams of common men," seems to engender the "romance" as exclusively masculine. But he nonetheless insists on quite antithetical characteristics: while any work of art in 1884 must be self-contained, rational, and emasculate, the novel of adventure appeals to "certain almost sensual and quite illogical tendencies in man" (12:214). We might plot Stevenson's aesthetic ideology on its manifest level as vacillating within the contraries of the "rational" and the "illogical," whose latent contradictions are, for Stevenson, "desire" and "the sensual." For Stevenson, as James himself sensed, Henry James's notion of "liberty" for the novel is indeed obese. Stevenson's notion of "liberty" in fiction, fueled by desire, is a contradictory formation, characterized by logic *and* irrationality, by the sensual *and* the strong. If the ideology of Besant's aesthetic, and his novel, merely restate an old-fashioned empiricist, middle-class complacency, while James's enacts a more sophisticated, "cultured" class position, then Stevenson's articulates in these values the contradictions at the heart of late Victorian capitalist ideology in general.

Thus while "A Humble Remonstrance" addresses the issues raised by James and Besant, it also picks up the polemic Stevenson had been engaged in for several years on behalf of "adventure" and "romance," guardedly (or "breathlessly")[68] criticizing realism. In 1883 he had written in Henley's *Magazine of Art* of "the fact which underlies a very dusty conflict of the critics" (his actual reference would seem to be to the contemporary controversy over "realism" provoked by Howells' essay "Henry James, Jr." in the *Century*). Stevenson presents the dusty conflict as traditionally between "realism" and "idealism," and then he deconstructs that opposition:

> All representative art, which can be said to live, is both realistic and ideal; and the realism about which we quarrel is a matter purely of externals. . . . This question of realism . . . regards not in the least degree the fundamental truth, but only the technical method, of a work of art. Be as ideal or as abstract as you please, you will be none the less veracious; but if you be weak, you run the risk of being tedious and inexpressive; and if you be very strong and honest, you may chance upon a masterpiece. (4:416–17)

In the strength and honesty (distinctly masculine virtues for Stevenson) of what he was to call, a year later, "desire," we can see his preference for adventure, or "romance."

He displays his aesthetic ideology, as we have seen, in his classification of the modes of fiction in "A Humble Remonstrance": the novel of adventure, the novel of character, and the dramatic novel. James obviously wrote "novels of character":

> he treats, for the most part, the statics of character, studying it at rest or only gently moved; and, with his usual delicate and just artistic instinct, he avoids those stronger passions which would deform the attitudes he loves to study, and change his sitters from the humourists of ordinary life to the brute forces and bare types of more emotional moments. (12:217)

The "dramatic novel," such as Meredith's *Rhoda Fleming* or Hardy's *A Pair of Blue Eyes*, is founded not on incident ("a strange and peculiarly English misconception" [12:218], but rather on passion:

> passion must appear upon the scene and utter its last word; passion
> is the be-all and the end-all, the plot and the solution, the pro-
> tagonist and the *deus ex machinâ* in one. (12:218)

In Stevenson's own preferred class of novel, that of adventure, the reader
puts aside judgment and is "submerged by the tale as by a billow"
(12:214). The author writes of "those things which he has only wished
to do." Any reader, even Henry James, has "ardently desired and fondly
imagined the details of such a life [say, treasure hunting] in youthful
day-dreams," and so the author of *Treasure Island*,

> counting upon that and well aware (cunning and low-minded man!)
> that this class of interest, having been frequently treated, finds a
> readily accessible and beaten road to the sympathies of the reader,
> addressed himself throughout to the building up and circumstantia-
> tion of this boyish dream. (12:215)

Stevenson's coyness here, preempting charges of authorial cunning and
low-mindedness, is a mark of the contradictions in his position, as the
"billow" is revealed to be a readily accessible and beaten road. Stevenson's house of fiction is here accommodating not only his own *Treasure
Island*, which, while popular like *All Sorts and Conditions of Men*, might
need to have a case made for it as *fine* art, but also the commercial,
indeed the entrepreneurial, ideology in late Victorian novel production. Hence Stevenson's emphasis on technique,[69] but also his insistence on the adventure novel or romance as an equivalent class of
novel to the novel of character and the dramatic novel.

    In October-November 1885, Stevenson offered *Strange Case of Dr.
Jekyll and Mr. Hyde* for serialization in *Longman's Magazine*. Longman
decided not to serialize it but instead to publish it in December in two
formats, a hard-cover volume at 1s. 6d. and in "fawn-coloured paper
wrappers, ornamented in blue, and lettered in red and blue" for 1s.[70]
Longman was to soften Stevenson's loss of immediate payment for the
serial by an advance payment of royalties on the first ten thousand copies
(Stevenson was to receive one-sixth of the retail price—2d. a copy), but,
in the event, publication and the royalty payment were deferred until
January 1886.[71] Graham Balfour, Stevenson's biographer, quotes Longman's account of the episode:

"The little book was printed," says Mr. Charles Longman, "but when it was ready the bookstalls were already full of Christmas numbers etc., and the trade would not look at it. We therefore withdrew it till after Christmas. In January it was launched—not without difficulty. The trade did not feel inclined to take it up, till a review appeared in the *Times* calling attention to the story. This gave it a start, and in the next six months close on forty thousand copies were sold in this country alone."[72]

Longman's account (as reported by Balfour) is so vague and cozy—"the bookstalls were full," so "the trade would not look at it"; then "the trade" did not want to "take it up" until after the *Times* had given it a good review—that we cannot know really what was at issue in December 1885. *Jekyll and Hyde* was published on 9 January 1886, with Scribner's American edition, from Longman's sheets and again in two formats, appearing on 8 January to forestall piracy, although the book was widely pirated.[73] Longman's advertised *Jekyll and Hyde* in the *Athenaeum* (and elsewhere) from 9 January until 3 April 1886. The favorable *Times* review (on 25 January 1886), praising "this sparsely printed little shilling volume," was quoted in the advertisement in the *Athenaeum* for 30 January. A blurb from the review in the *Academy*, noting that *Jekyll and Hyde* was "weirdly imaginative" and "could be read with ease in a couple of hours," was added on 27 February. On 3 April the *Times* notice was dropped and to the *Academy* blurb was added one from the *Whitehall Review*—"The reader scarcely breathes while the course of the story proceeds"—and one from the *Graphic*:

> This book is not to be recommended to readers of a nervous temperament, seated in lonely rooms, during the small hours of the night.[74]

It would seem from their advertising that Longman's quickly supplemented the *Times*'s good word with more sensational advertising, perhaps because of the sermons being preached about the novel; after all, the *Academy* reviewer had also thought *Jekyll and Hyde* "worthy of Hawthorne," but this was not mentioned.

As Harold Orel put it, "Stevenson always wanted to write commercially, and often succeeded."[75] *Jekyll and Hyde* was especially successful in the United States; Balfour suggested in 1901 that "probably not less than a quarter of a million copies in all have been sold in the United States."[76] But the "Chace Act" did not take effect before Stevenson's death in 1894 and he benefited little financially, for the popularity of *Jekyll and Hyde* is best indicated by its seven pirate publishers between 1886 and 1891, who sold the novel for 10 to 25 cents a copy (Scribner's clothbound edition sold for 1 dollar, the paperback for 25 cents).[77] In 1887, *Scribner's Magazine* tried to combat the pirates of Stevenson's work, exhorting "admirers of his genius" not to buy pirated editions,[78] and one effect of this may have been to inspire Harper's, a pirate, suddenly to offer Stevenson a £20 royalty on a volume containing *Treasure Island, Jekyll and Hyde*, and *Kidnapped*. Stevenson haughtily turned the check over to Scribner's and published the correspondence in the *Times*:

> Since I have been in the hands of Messrs. Charles Scribners Sons I have received a substantial annual sum from my books in the United States, and Messrs. Harper, by this act of piracy, and above all by printing my three most popular books in one, cut off this income at the root.[79]

With *Jekyll and Hyde*, Scribner's became Stevenson's authorized American publisher. In 1887 there was a month of discussion in which Stevenson and Longman's insisted that Scribner's pay Longman's half the royalties for *Jekyll and Hyde*, since Longman's still held the American book rights. Scribner's reluctantly acceded, although there is a memorandum in the Longman's archive from Longman's office in New York claiming that the dispute and considerable correspondence resulted in Longman's "relinquishing the American market to Mr. Stevenson."[80] This scramble indicates, at the very least, the popularity of *Jekyll and Hyde*:

> Within a short time the names of Jekyll and Hyde, if not Stevenson's own, were known everywhere in the English-speaking world; the story became a popular topic in the press and the subject of countless sermons, one of which was delivered at St. Paul's, and of serious articles in religious periodicals; it was translated into a number of different languages, and adapted for the stage in several countries.[81]

And when the Stevensons landed in New York on 7 September 1887, they were met by a crowd of reporters.[82]

One determinate effect, in the late 1880s, of Stevenson's popularity
was that "Stevenson was the first modern novelist to be assiduously
pursued by collectors"; Barry Menikoff writes that, after Stevenson's
death, "it appeared his writing was being promoted simply to drive up
auction prices."[83] This process was visible very early: J. H. Slater's
Early Editions, published the year of Stevenson's death, valued the first
edition of *Jekyll and Hyde* at 7s., an appreciation of almost 500 percent
in eight years; in his 1914 *Bibliography*, Slater valued it at 26s.[84] A
more insidious effect of Stevenson's popularity was the appearance at
auction in May 1897 of Wise's forgery (which fetched £14) of his
pamphlet *The Thermal Influence of Forests*, followed in June 1897 by
Some College Memories (1886) and, in 1899, *The Story of a Lie* (1882).[85]
The creation of a rare book market in Stevenson's books and a parasite
market in forgeries was a function of Stevenson's popularity and his
early death, but also of the complications of his life and writing:

> he would engage himself in as many projects as he could, maximiz-
> ing his profits as quickly as possible. He would arbitrarily raise his
> royalty rate, and when that was insufficient he would renounce
> royalty arrangements altogether and agree only to the outright sale
> of his copyrights.[86]

His relations with publishers were often managed from a distance
through his friends Charles Baxter and Sidney Colvin, and as we have
seen, in the production of *Jekyll and Hyde* as with "The Beach at Falesá,"
"he supplied the art: a variety of producers were envolved in its finish-
ing, marketing, and distribution."[87] The same short life of hurry and
travel which fed the romantic myth of Robert Louis Stevenson enforced
the awkward and alienated production of his books; in turn, the complexity of their publishing history, and its scattered agents, invited the
sort of false history and invented provenance at which T. J. Wise was
so adept. While *Jekyll and Hyde* was never forged, the pauses and hiatuses
of its production, and the quick, entrepreneurial sensationalizing in
its distribution, created the kind of international commodity which
might easily be exploited in ways legal and illegal.

    Strange Case of Dr. Jekyll and Mr. Hyde provides an instance of the
potential for entrepreneurial (and extra-entrepreneurial) exploitation
in Robert Louis Stevenson's idea of romance. In 1887 Henry James
remarked of Stevenson's fiction, and *Jekyll and Hyde* in particular, that

Stevenson "achieves his best effects without the aid of the ladies," [88] and Elaine Showalter has recently added more pointedly that "*Jekyll and Hyde* is about communities of men." [89] It is this absence of women, allowing the foregrounding of a masculine community, which indicates the location of *Jekyll and Hyde* within the ideological structure which I have analyzed in "A Humble Remonstrance" and that is also to be found among Stevenson's other literary essays of the early 1880s. For this is a *specific* community; these are "all intelligent reputable men, and all judges of good wine." [90] The male, professional clubman's social structure in the story realistically presents "a certain artificial series of impressions," and the ideology of this series is what we plotted as, for Stevenson, "romance." The genial respectability is linked in a single sentence to the contradictory "sea of liberty" in which Mr. Hyde bathes (86). *Jekyll and Hyde*'s atmosphere of danger and fear, seized upon in all its significant simplicity by the publishers, is only the symptom of a more complex position, a "sane and customary" order of life (35), rational yet illogical, requiring (for "meaning") the co-presence of the sensual and of desire. Here is the return of "the feminine," which the masculine community in the text ostensibly excludes, and here also is the general late Victorian capitalist ideology at the heart of Stevenson's idea of "romance."

Henry James was to say that Stevenson "leaves so wide a margin for the wonderful—it impinges with easy assurance upon the text—that he escapes the danger of being brought up by cases he has not allowed for. When he allows for Mr. Hyde he allows for everything." [91] It is precisely Hyde's surplusage of signification—the exact nature of Hyde's sensual excesses is never specified, and Stevenson denied the more obvious speculations—which defines *Jekyll and Hyde* as romance in Stevenson's aesthetic. If Hyacinth Robinson was someone upon whom nothing was lost, there is, from Stevenson's perspective, truly a kind of patrician "obesity" about Hyacinth. In Jekyll's alter ego, on the other hand, Stevenson "allows for everything," not just everything perceptible and appreciable, but everything *imaginable*; Hyde as *imagined*, indeed as *imagination*, illogical and sensual, escapes from the community of these men, a bourgeois community "to whom the fanciful was the immodest" (35), to a world of unspecified, because nonspecific, exchange. Henry Jekyll's full statement of the case, in which he reveals his scientific discovery, a "tincture" which "shook the very fortress of identity" or, again, "shook the doors of the prisonhouse of my disposition" (83, 85), is far from being an overly realistic intrusion or a "mistake" in the story, or even simply a historically appropriate "'scientific' explanation for everything that, up to that point in the tale, had been manifested symbolically."[92] In the ideology of the text it is an instance of that self-confident scientific rationalism which of necessity overdetermines the novel as a romance. "Released from the common sense of his neighbors and the truths of the sociologists,"[93] Mr. Hyde yet has meaning only in relation to Dr. Jekyll, Mr. Utterson, and the other "onlookers."[94] "My two natures," says Jekyll, "had memory in common" (89), the sign of their dialectical bond in Stevenson's ideology of romance, like an expected surprise.

Strange Case of Dr. Jekyll and Mr. Hyde thus presents not a picture to compete with life, but a certain artificial series of impressions, a representation of the imaginary relationship of bourgeois males to their real conditions of existence.[95] Its manifest binary opposition, between a respectable Jekyll and a degenerate Hyde, was immediately exploitable to an audience which might enjoy reading it in lonely rooms, during the small hours of the night. But the text's subversion of that binary in the interest of Stevensonian "romance" spoke also to the mass readership of the late 1880s, especially perhaps in the United States. "Desire," while taking its purchase in the sane and customary order of life, while also pressing determinedly into the undefined and unrestricted fullness of sensual life, is the necessary psychic position of entrepreneurial ideology, producing the contradictions, the "conflicts of interest," the black markets, launderings, embezzlements, and sophisticated control which characterize the modern capitalist social formation. Jekyll and Hyde was, not surprisingly, a successful venture in entrepreneurial publishing. It is a symptomatic text within the modern social formation.

If "the familiar" in Besant's novel is bourgeois and comfortable, and its working-class world made so too, then James's novel attempts something else, to explore, or "perambulate," the consciousness of the London working class, the limitations of its "experience" (in James's sense of the word), and its possible expansion by contact with familiar high culture. In Stevenson, *everything* is familiar, because in "romance" everything is imaginable; the exotic on every level becomes familiar and can become a commodity. And if, as I have said, the "preconstituted" discourse in All Sorts and Conditions of Men is transversed, so to speak, at a very acute angle, in The Princess Casamassima the transverse discourse of high Victorian taste encounters the preconstituted at a somewhat less acute angle, becoming awkwardly and indecisively another version of the familiar, of Arnold and Ruskin. In *Jekyll and Hyde*, however, the "angle" between the preconstituted and its "original," "innovative" transverse discourse is so *obtuse*, so opened out by the assertion of Hyde's radical, unspecified depravity, that the "transverse" becomes simply the vaguely *opposite*, and we infer Hyde's depravity only from its alleged difference from the familiar propriety of Jekyll and the others.

But I do not want to conclude this chapter with this rather formalist analysis, however much I believe in its validity. We have been reading, not simply three novels, but "novel production in the 1880s," and I have tried to present an analysis which, first of all, runs counter to two opposed understandings of novel production: that novels simply and straightforwardly enact an authorial ideology, or that they simply and straightforwardly enact the ideology of "their time." It should be clear that none of these three novels can be adequately described as the result or practice of a particular authorial ideology, a specific set of ideas about "the art of fiction." Besant, most obviously, fails to demonstrate the validity of a "scientific," positivist conception of novel production, but *The Princess Casamassima*, too, makes a poor case for James's beliefs in the liberty and autonomy of novelist and novel, suggesting rather the unacknowledged radical uncertainty at the heart of the novelist's "liberty." Stevenson's effort at a more libertine liberty only demonstrates the hollowness, or windiness, of his formulations about "romance" throughout the early eighties, just as the necessary rationality and science of Dr. Jekyll always restrict as they define the exemplary libertinism of Mr. Hyde.

And it is here especially, and in *Jekyll and Hyde* in particular, that we can see the poverty of the other understandings of novel production I have referred to. I have not been arguing that what I have called the ideology of the text is produced autonomously by the text of *Strange Case of Dr. Jekyll and Mr. Hyde*, as a revelation (even subconscious) of contemporary social ideology. Rather, the ideology of the text I have been examining is historically produced, as the physical text is itself produced, and in the same process. Just as the policies and practices of Chatto and Windus, and the professional practices of Walter Besant within the structure of late Victorian publishing as a whole, along with innumerable other determinations (such as the class struggle in

London's East End), produced in 1883–84 *All Sorts and Conditions of Men* as itself a distinct ideological practice for its readers, so Macmillan's and the *Atlantic Monthly*, and the advantages and disadvantages of James's transnational status, as well as revolutionary politics in the eighties and innumerable other conditions, determined that strange ideological practice which is *The Princess Casamassima*: a text which is literally produced "internationally" by its two formats. So too, the more specifically, if general, capitalist ideology of *Strange Case of Dr. Jekyll and Mr. Hyde* is produced, not as a simple reflection of turn-of-the-century capitalism, but as an ideological practice, the reader's experience of a determinate textual structure, determined, that is, by the exigencies of the production relations in which Robert Louis Stevenson found himself, but also by the interplay of entrepreneurial publishing with not only the market for novels but the market, in the 1880s and 1890s, for books as rarities, as a particular other sort of commodity.

Finally, so little is the ideology of each of these texts simply the author's doing, or, again, simply the expression of its "time," that none can even be begun to be read except in relation to the others, and to other eighties novels I have not discussed (or read). But each must also be read against the structured interplay in late Victorian publishing, the tension between the entrepreneurial and the list publisher which in turn structures the market for novels. The narrative uncertainty, or constitutive self-division, at the heart of *The Princess Casamassima* is in part determined by the tension between the American magazine serial mode of publication and Macmillan's conservative British list mode. The determinate entrepreneurial relations of the production of *All Sorts and Conditions of Men* are sufficiently obvious, and their influence in Longman's production of *Jekyll and Hyde* only slightly less so—it would be nice to know what Longman's discussed among themselves in November/December 1885. But these specific determinations arising from the historical structures of publishing are imbricated in ideologies of value like those we have discussed, determining what is published, and how, by certain popular practices. Henry James's refusal to name his hundred best books, it might be argued, determines in a small part the text of *The Princess Casamassima*, as does more obviously his particular coign of vantage within the developing system of international copyright. *All Sorts and Conditions of Men*, a very British novel as we have seen, seems to have been simply left, internationally, to the pirates. Stevenson's place in those practices was different, or rather his publishers' attention to different markets and their copyright practices differed from the publishing habits of Macmillan regarding James. It is in Stevenson's novel, in its structure and themes, *and* in its overdetermination by the necessities of Stevenson's ménage, that we can see the traces of the patriarchal/capitalist literary mode of production. The text of each novel is marked by these differential determinations and by others. This complex intertextuality, some of which we have explored but most of which we inevitably have not, is what might be called "novel publishing in the Eighties," the production of fiction seen (or striven to be seen) in its fullest historical context.

4. The Process of Literary Capital in the 1890s
Caine, Corelli, and Bennett

D ESPITE the close attention we have been paying
to empirical details of publishing history and
literary ideology, the meanings of these materials
clearly do not reside *in* them, there for the picking; their "meaning,"
as I hope my approach has demonstrated, is *dialectical*, symptomatic
of determinate historical processes. From time to time, following Bourdieu, I have introduced "objectivist" generalizations, or what Althusser
called "empirical concepts," general concepts which bear "on the *fact*
that such a social formation presents such and such a configuration,
traits, particular arrangements, which characterize it as *existing*."[1]
Empirical concepts such as the "list"/"entrepreneurial" contradiction
thus identify particular arrangements in late Victorian publishing
which characterize it as existing. But we are also attempting to theorize
dialectically the structure which these objectivist concepts identify,
and to recognize it as *capital*, indicating the mode of its historical
existence.

I want now to look closely at two controversies of the early nineties:
the debate over "romance" and "realism," which displaces the "art of
fiction" debate of the eighties, and the discussion of what was called
in 1890 "candor in fiction." I want to emphasize that I am examining
the transformations of a continuing historical process, the restructuring
of publishing capital; while I move from a discussion of literary events
in the eighties to one of literary events in the nineties, I do not mean
to suggest historical "stages," to fetishize those decades. I am using the
language of "decades" to locate temporally the events, but I want to
shed its ideological baggage. In 1928 William Frierson attempted to

"mark the stages of the change," from "indignation at the crudities" of foreign realism to a more sympathetic feeling toward Zola beginning in 1893. Frierson selected 1893 as "the pivotal year in the orientation of English taste in fiction," and some years later Kenneth Graham suggested 1887 as the turning point for romance. But if we see the orientation historically, in relation to a continuing, self-adjusting process (one of the restructuring of publishing capital), the preoccupation with a single year is irrelevant. Even were a distinct shift in "feeling" or "taste" easy to demonstrate, Frierson admits that realistic novels "vied with the romantic novels of adventure for popularity between the years 1885 and 1890," achieving only "a partial victory . . . for the principle of realism."[2] The realism/romance debate of the eighties and early nineties clearly presents only an imaginary understanding of the current situation in British fiction and so must be read only as a symptom of the larger change. The Besant/James/Stevenson "art of fiction" debate of 1884 has become more complex, has been de- (or re-) composed, so to speak, amidst the overdeterminations I have described. Nor was the "candor in fiction" debate significant in itself, as, say, a historical stage toward some greater candor or truthfulness in fiction overall (as we approach the blazing truthfulness of present-day writing), but is rather, along with the realism/romance controversy, symptomatic of the larger historical transformation, alluding to its configuration or traits. Amidst the crucial negotiations over international copyright, for instance, but on the level of aesthetic ideology, the imagined issue between realism and romance and the question of candor assert that there is also a local crisis in novel production.

Just as in Chapter 2 we read this conjunctural crisis on its economic level as a tension between "list" and "entrepreneurial" publishers, so we can read it here on the level of aesthetic ideology as debates over realism, romance, and candor. In these ideological struggles, "publishing" worked out an accommodation between residual ideologies and the necessities of the emerging literary mode of production. By the early nineties, these issues had become urgent questions of material practice: that is, what publishing practices best accommodate or contain realistic *or* romantic ideology or, alternatively, what synthetic aesthetic ideology might best serve the commodity-text of the new patriarchal/ capitalist literary mode of production? Neither realism nor romance (and certainly not candor) was simply the ideological "expression" of a new patriarchal/capitalist publishing sector. With new participants—

Andrew Lang, George Saintsbury and others (it is significant that the debate is taken over from the novelists by critics and reviewers)—the discussion begun by Howells in 1882 and developed by Besant, James, and Stevenson in 1884 continues on a changed terrain. Stevenson's energetic partisanship of romance in 1884, in particular his strenuous attempt at a redefinition of romantic freedom, and above all the popular success of his own novels changed the stakes in the debate—"to Stevenson we owe the recrudescence of the historical romance."[3] But these aesthetic issues overlap and interact with the economic; they mark the terrain on which the conjunctural crisis is worked through, their real meaning demanding a dialectical reading. I shall begin mine with the new form which the "art of fiction" debate takes.

"Romance," in the late eighties and nineties, was not simply a "turn-of-the-century vogue,"[4] but the ideology of the fictional practice of Robert Louis Stevenson and Rider Haggard which, with its assumed contrary, realism, overdetermined the restructuring of publishing. On its latent level, as we have seen, the debate in its earlier phase engaged not only the literal or factual necessities of capitalism in general, but also "idealism," those various ideological positions, metaphysical and scientific, from which this empiricism was resisted and opposed.[5] This is the ideological terrain upon which the debate was fought out, as the publishing sector produced and discovered the determinate ideology of its patriarchal/capitalist literary mode of production. Graham's suggestion that 1887 was "the year of recognition for the new romance,"[6] since in that year Saintsbury, Rider Haggard, and Andrew Lang all published essays on the romance, makes the wrong emphasis. *Poole's Index* records two other, anonymous, essays on the romance in 1887, one of them a direct response to Haggard which used the "new novelist," Hall Caine, as a case. But in 1888 there was another, and another in 1889, and there were four more in 1890, including Caine's essay on romance as "the cry of the time," and Edmund Gosse's call for a "new aim" in fiction, "a concession to the human instinct for mystery and beauty." Two more essays appeared in 1891, after which, suddenly, it would seem that "romance," or "the romance," was no longer a topic for critical discussion.[7] Significantly, Andrew Lang, in his "'Tendencies' in Fiction" in the *North American Review* in 1895, while claiming that the novel has become "a more and more potent literary engine," nowhere mentions the romance.[8] Thus the brevity and form of this efflorescence put in question the simple "recognition" of

romance in 1887, as does the diversity of the pairings in which
"romance" was cast in these periodical essays: narrowness/breadth,
familiar/unfamiliar, romance/Darwinism, psychology/supernaturalism.
These essays on the romance merely attest to the general currency of
a discussion which the more prominent critics focused and channeled.

For the essays by Haggard, Lang, and Saintsbury in 1887 do indicate
the new ideological terrain of the realism/romance debate. Rider Haggard's pedestrian essay on romance in the *Contemporary Review* for
February 1887, starts with the assertion that the love of romance is
"probably coeval with the existence of humanity," thus modestly deper-
sonalizing the success of *King Solomon's Mines* (1885) and *She* (1887)
while universalizing the appeal of romance. Haggard's essay contrasts
"those works of fancy which appeal . . . to all time and humanity at
large" to three other "schools" of fiction: the "new American school"
of "laboured nothingness," the Naturalistic school ("of which Zola is
high priest . . . an accursed thing"), and "the ordinary popular English
novel [which] represents life as it is considered desirable that school-
girls should suppose it to be." All of this is placed in a discourse of "yearly
output," "publishing as a trade" and "the market," "demand for books"
and "piracy." Haggard's "romance" seeks "the paths and calm retreats
of pure imagination," "the great profound beyond." What is wanted in
English fiction "is a higher ideal and more freedom to work it out"—a
"moderate and proper freedom," to be sure:

> Art in the purity of its idealized truth should resemble some perfect
> Greek statue. It should be cold but naked, and looking thereon men
> should be led to think of nought but beauty.[9]

Haggard's ideal of romance is a constellation of the values we have
discussed earlier: a constant awareness of novels as commodities, a belief
in the "really great," a certain view of women and the candor appropriate in sexual matters, and a sense of "American" competition.
"Romance," not to mention "the great profound beyond," best accom-
modates these values, he implies. Andrew Lang's essay in the November
1887 *Contemporary Review* uses the metaphor not of the marketplace
but of a battle, and he sees fiction as a shield with two sides: "the study
of manners and of character, on the one hand; on the other, the description of adventure, the delight of romantic narrative." While affect-
ing a democratic tolerance of either mode, Lang dismisses "realism"

in favor of "stories told for the story's sake," because, he says, "the bar-
baric element has not died out of our blood":

> Not for nothing did Nature leave us all savages under our white
> skins; she has wrought thus that we might have many delights,
> among others "the joy of adventurous living," and of reading about
> adventurous living.

The savage within us, Lang claims, "calls out for more news about the
fight with the Apache, or Piute, who killed the soldier-man," and he
ends his essay, famously:

> if the battle between the crocodile of Realism and the catawampus
> of Romance is to be fought out to the bitter end—why, in that
> Ragnarôk, I am on the side of the catawampus.[10]

Saintsbury discussed the state of the English novel in the September
Fortnightly (and the state of the French novel four months later).[11] His
vantage point is thus more comprehensive than Lang's or Haggard's
while (even in the section on the French novel) decidedly British, and
his sense of the best in literature is so acute (while so diffuse) that he
can claim that English novelists have, in recent years, "greatly bettered
the *average*—(I must be pardoned italics here)—the average structure
and arrangement of the average novel." He dismisses William Dean
Howells as a "virtuous beginner," with "those comic little critical excur-
sions of his." Saintsbury constructs a brief history of English fiction
as an alternation between "the pure romance" and the "analytic novel";
by this last he means "minute manners-painting and refined character
analysis." Like Lang and Haggard, he is on the side of the catawampus,
welcoming "that return to the pure romance . . . , which was seen
to be coming several years ago." "The reappearance of the romance
of adventure," he writes, is not at all likely to be "a mere passing
phenomenon":

> For the romance is of its nature eternal and preliminary to the
> novel. The novel is of its nature transitory and is parasitic on the
> romance. If some of the examples of novels themselves partake of
> eternity, it is only because the practitioners have been cunning
> enough to borrow much from the romance.

Saintsbury also introduces the matter of "candor," sneering at "that curious scholasticism of dull uncleanness on which too many French novelists spend their time." He feels that "the 'cult of the young person' which some innocent British writers deplore, has at least kept us from the last depth of dirty dulness." In his January 1888 continuation of the essay, he attributes the decline of the French novel to "the absence of consideration for the young person." [12]

These three essays, by a popular romance writer, an editor and puff writer, and a schoolteacher ("King Saintsbury," in 1895 to succeed Masson as professor of English Literature in Edinburgh),[13] appeared in 1887 in monthlies characterized, the *Wellesley Index* says, by liberal rationalism (the *Fortnightly*) and by "broad, evangelical, semi-socialistic liberalism" (the *Contemporary*);[14] these are progressive monthly papers. The three essayists, no strangers to each other (or to Stevenson), argue forcefully in their different ways that the romance of adventure, Stevenson's romance, and Haggard's, is the literary mode of the future. Reacting to realism, these essays go beyond mere "recognition" of romance to that sort of diffuse, broadly motivated promotion which has come to characterize literary journalism, where personal interest and a reading of the history of taste happen wonderfully to coincide. Thus at the same time as the patriarchal/capitalist literary mode of production is producing its appropriate general ideologies of literary value, so it is producing its particular aesthetic ideology, an amalgam of realism and the romantic "yearning for escape," [15] which was to serve its transformed production of novels.

By the nineties this discussion was clearly linked to that on the bounds of propriety in the novel; the signifier "Zola" was common to both. The two debates, as debates, produce their ideologies in very different ways. Rather than the field generated in the realism/romance debate ("realism/romance:empiricism/idealism"), here it is a matter of "candor/hypocrisy:freedom/censorship." The realism/romance debate constantly acknowledged in ways we have noted that it is about the *production* of novels, although it displaced this knowledge, as we have seen, into a discussion of the creative imagination, ostensibly addressing the aesthetic issues dividing the two literary modes. The *New Review* essays we will consider now, on the other hand, present "candor" in fiction as an issue in the market or audience, displacing novel *production* into *distribution*. Whereas the positions taken in the candor essays, as we shall see, may be either "emancipating" or repressive, the whole discourse of "candor" has to do only with ways of shaping and broadening the market for novels. This occludes the crucial issue of the place of women as *producers* and in the publishing apparatus. The "candor in fiction" debate constructs women only as *consumers* of fiction: trivialized as "the Young Person," women are inconceivable as serious producers of novels. This position structures publishing as protective and paternal, as a *patriarchal*/capitalist literary mode of production.

For while each author in the *New Review* symposium discusses "candor" in a different way, each accepts "candor," "the realm of experience open to the novel," [16] as the issue. Walter Besant writes of the author ("he") and society in his usual moralizing terms, Linton writes of the British Matron as "the true censor of the Press" (10) and Hardy talks of "the unending flow of invention" and historical process (15). Hardy, not surprisingly, comes closest to an idea of a determinate production process, but he cannot, of course, see "patriarchy" as among the historical determinations. Besant is the least subtle, easily accepting the status quo. He locates the authority for censorship in "Average Opinion"—"Average Opinion cannot be resisted"—but he bases his claims for its authority on dubious grounds. Since the Average Briton knows that "the cultured class" of British women are entirely to be trusted, the topics of sexual license, infidelity, etc., characteristic of French novels, are simply irrelevant (8–9). Eliza Lynn Linton takes another tack; while Linton felt that contemporary novelists had a more limited choice than before among racial, religious, political, and class topics, she attributed the "pitiable poverty of the ordinary novel" to the "wearisome repetition of the same themes," and the current popularity of romances to their "not pretending to deal with life as it is" (10). Linton dealt more concretely than Besant with the apparatuses of book distribution, noting that while the writer who "ventures into the forbidden Garden of Roses will be boycotted by respectable booksellers and libraries," he (*sic*) may achieve large sales "surreptitiously" (11). Linton resolves the contradiction between the "young Person" and "faithful representation of the realities of human life" (13) by advocating the father's locked bookcase for novels that deal with "life as it is":

We have the queer anomaly of a strong-headed and masculine
nation cherishing a feeble, futile, milk-and-water literature. (14)

"The locked bookcase," she writes, "is better" (14).

Thus "the Young Person," for both Besant and Linton, is the stalking-horse of patriarchal authority. Hardy, in contrast, claims to find a more general law than the Name of the Father. "Even imagination," he begins, "is the slave of stolid circumstance" (15), and both terms of his formula, "imagination" and "circumstance," dictate that his argument should deal more closely with the *production* of novels. The "looped orbit" of evolution, of course, structures Hardy's argument—"Things move in cycles," "the periodicity which marks the course of taste," "originality makes scores of failures for one final success" (16)—but the "upward advance" of "conscientious fiction," he writes, has been diverted by the "lateral advance" of magazine and circulating library (17). Magazine serials and Mudie's are the vehicles of what Hardy calls "the self-consciousness engendered by interference with spontaneity" (18), and he then ponders the task of reforming those institutions. While he believes it unlikely that the existing magazine and book-lending system would brook any great modification, he recommends a radical change in book distribution:

> a system of publication under which books could be bought and not borrowed, when they would naturally resolve themselves into classes instead of being, as now, made to wear a common livery in style and subject, enforced by their supposed necessities in addressing indiscriminately a general audience. (20–21)

Here Hardy, like Linton but unlike Besant, looks for a solution in "discrimination," in specialized audiences, but rather than father's locked bookcase, Hardy would enforce it by new forms of distribution. For example, novels might be included as in France as *feuilletons* in newspapers or magazines exclusively for adults (21). Hardy's suggestion that novels be bought rather than borrowed, of course, would necessitate precisely what he could not see: the transformation of the literary mode of production which Macmillan's net book scheme would initiate within that very year.

This discussion of candor in fiction in the *New Review* in 1890—a new 6d. monthly whose aim, "commercial rather than literary," was "to outstrip even the half-crown reviews [the *Fortnightly* and *Nineteenth Century*] not so much in quality as in profits, through a large volume of sales" [17]—both contributes to and is symptomatic of the transformation of the literary mode of production. The three essayists' overriding preoccupation with young women readers in a symposium on *candor*, coupled with their varied consciousness of the contradiction in allowing independent distributors to censor, together raise the possibility of a self-censoring mode of publication. This set of linked assumptions draws upon the assumptions of the contemporaneous realism/romance debate, and helps determine ideologically the new patriarchal/capitalist literary mode of production. We can see these linkages, or overdeterminations, most clearly in Saintsbury's revision and expansion in 1892 of his 1887 essay on realism/romance.

1. An indication of the historical change on another level is the welcome given "a new novelist," Hall Caine, by a *Westminster* reviewer in October 1887. The writer places Caine's first two novels in the midst of the current debates, noting that they rejected Howells/James realism, "the morbid indulgence of finical self-introspection": "Both his published fictions afford evidence . . . calculated to count as a potent factor in the prevailing romantic movement," with "no line of them unfit for the purest eye, no sentiment that would not grace the most fleckless manhood." Most significantly, the reviewer detects in Caine's novels an attempt to temper romance with realism, or vice versa:

> Mr Caine's romance is the romance of reality . . . , that combination of the familiar with the unfamiliar, that blending of the commonplace with the unusual, which must ever remain the essence of the highest romantic achievement.[18]

Closely linked to the rise of Caine's reputation was William Heinemann's emergence as one of "the new imprints" at the end of the eighties,[19] and I want to examine that interplay, the establishment of the new publisher and the production of his first best-seller, together. Heinemann would seem personally to have been the embodiment of entrepreneurial attitudes. His biographers speak of his "audacity" and "enterprise": "he was tough, cosmopolitan, cultivated, successful in business and had immense energy and single-mindedness."[20] Be that as it may, the success of the production of Hall Caine's *The Bondman* is an instance of the overdetermination of a text and its production in the entrepreneurial mode.

On 29 May 1887, Caine signed a memorandum of agreement giving Tillotson's Fiction Bureau the exclusive serial copyright to *The Bondman*, his fourth novel, for £400. Caine was to provide the novel in the usual three-volume format, in twenty-four installments of 6,000 words each, and Tillotson's were to arrange publication commencing before 3 March 1889 in their own *Bolton Weekly Journal* and other newspapers around Britain, and to supply advance sheets to an American publisher to secure copyright there. Caine delivered the first five installments by 1 August 1888 and the rest in weekly installments until the end of serialization in 1889.[21] On 1 January 1890, William Heinemann, "for ten years associated with the late firm of Trübner & Co.," announced that he had commenced business as a publisher of works in every branch of literature and that "a first list of forthcoming Publications, including works by some of the leading writers of the day, will shortly be issued."[22] The *Athenaeum* announced on 18 January that in early February Heinemann would issue *Hauntings: Fantastic Stories*, by Vernon Lee, and two single-volume novels, F. W. Robinson's *A Very Strange Family* and Elizabeth Stuart Phelps's *Come Forth!* Heinemann's own advertisement in the same issue added:

> The BONDMAN. A New Saga. By Hall Caine. Author of "The Deemster." In 3 vols. At all Libraries on February 1.

On 1 February, Heinemann inserted a note reminding *Athenaeum* readers again that Hall Caine's *The Bondman* was "This day at all Libraries."[23] Towards the end of 1889, Caine had offered *The Bondman* to Cassell. He was interviewed there by the chief editor and the publishing manager, who told him that the novel was too "gloomy." Caine argued that it was not more so than *A Tale of Two Cities* or *Wuthering Heights*, which had sold well, and they responded that his asking price, £400 outright, was too high. Caine then offered the novel to Heinemann, who paid him, Heinemann's biographer was told, "£300 down on account of adequate royalties, and both author and publisher made a great many thousands out of it."[24] The commodity-text *The Bondman* is the record of that making, and I now want to trace that production process in the literary periodicals and between the covers of the novel.

On 8 February 1890, Heinemann advertised that

> the First Edition of Mr. Hall Caine's New Saga, "THE BONDMAN,"
> 3 vols., has been disposed of within a week of publication, and a Second Edition (now in active preparation) will be at all Libraries early next week.

The advertisement also quoted from the novel's first review, in the *Scotsman* for 3 February: "In this new work [Caine] . . . has placed himself beyond the front rank of the novelists of the day."[25] The same issue of the *Athenaeum* carried its own brief review of the book (176), and a month later Heinemann's advertisement, again for *The Bondman* alone, quoted another phrase from the *Scotsman*—"fit to rank with the most powerful fiction of the past century"—along with notices from thirteen more newspapers and weekly magazines: "masterpiece," "a strenuous and sustained imaginative effort," "almost Homeric power."[26] On 8 March, the *Times* published its laudatory review (15), which Heinemann quoted a week later when he announced a third edition. Heinemann's 8 March advertisement included for the first time Gladstone's comments on the novel—"freshness," "vigor," "sustained interest," "integrity of aim"—a puff which, the *Academy* reviewer objected, the "splendid novel . . . does not need,"[27] and on 25 October, a mere eight months after *The Bondman* was published as a three-decker, Heinemann brought out the Cheap (Fourth) Edition," in one volume at 3s. 6d., advertising it in the new year as the "Best Novel for Holiday Reading."[28]

But the history of *The Bondman*'s first year includes other events. In April, while *The Bondman* was still available only in three volumes (at 31s. 6d.), Hall Caine published a critical article, "The New Watchwords of Fiction," in the *Contemporary Review*; the watchwords, he said, "for the next twenty years at least," were to be "ROMANTICISM AND IDEALISM," for "*Fiction is not nature, it is not character, it is not imagined history; it is fallacy, poetic fallacy, pathetic fallacy. . . .*"[29] Also, Heinemann inaugurated in May his first major publishing enterprise, his "International Library," translations of works by continental authors. A recent history of William Heinemann, Ltd., suggests that the apparent eclecticism of the 1890–93 lists is deceptive:

> steadily a clearer structure emerges, based on fiction, aimed principally at the subscription libraries, balanced by heavyweight series for the most part thought up and commissioned in the office.[30]

The International Library's first three volumes, in paper at 2s. 6d. or limp cloth at 3s. 6d., were a novel by Bjornstjerne Bjornson, Maupassant's *Pierre and Jean*, and *The Chief Justice* by Emil Franzos. Edmund Gosse was the editor of the new series, and his prospectus places it squarely in the midst of the current ideological compromise. The International Library, like *The Bondman*, aspires to "romance" and "realism" together. While "there is no continental country," Gosse proclaims, "that has not, within the last half-century, felt the dew of revival on the threshing-floor of its worn-out schools of romance," nevertheless, "in almost every language, too, this movement has tended to display itself more and more in the direction of what is reported and less of what is created." And although "life is now treated in fiction by every race but our own with singular candour, . . . it is not difficult . . . to discard all which may justly give offense."[31] Heinemann's first major publishing venture, then, while designed to compete with Tauschnitz abroad,[32] was thus nicely calculated also to attract a contemporary British audience.

These entrepreneurial impulses dictated, too, the discourses by which *The Bondman* was promoted. One of his lifelong friends told Frederic Whyte, Heinemann's biographer, that Heinemann "was interested in the display side of advertisements and wrappers, but less in their contents,"[33] and this interest shows in the firm's advertisements, as *The Bondman* was made a best-seller. The quotations from reviews and Gladstone's puff were fairly conventional additions, but other aspects of the display side of the advertisements for *The Bondman* indicate their entrepreneurial thrust. The advertisement which announces that the one-volume edition is "Now Ready at all Booksellers" is laid out in a vertical column in the middle of the *Athenaeum* page. The title, *The Bondman*, is repeated sixteen times, one beneath the other, alternating with reviewers' comments down the page. This is a larger version of, say, Spencer Blackett's notice for their "Monsieur Judas. By the Author of the 'Mystery of a Hansom Cab'" in the 28 March *Athenaeum*, and it mimics the style of such advertisements as those for "Carter's Little Liver Pills" or "Elliman's Universal Embrocation" in the daily press.[34] The "display" of each of these advertisements on its page is distinctly strident. Similarly entrepreneurial is the discourse of production figures which Heinemann's advertisements for *The Bondman* adopted after its publication in a single volume in October ("Tenth Thousand"), measuring out the year in thousands: 15 November ("Eleventh Thousand"), 6 December ("Twelfth Thousand"), 3 January 1891 ("Thirteenth Thousand"); the Twenty-sixth thousand was announced on 28 July 1894.[35] This was a promotional discourse favored by Richard Bentley, who, for example, announced in March 1891 a new edition of Mrs Henry Woods's thirty-four novels ("Sale upwards of a Million copies") by giving the publication figures for each, from *East Lynne* ("Two Hundred and Twenty-fifth Thousand") to *Pomeroy Abbey* ("Twenty-first Thousand").[36] But Heinemann announces the sales figures as publication proceeds. His entrepreneurial publishing practice thus shows in the forms of "display" by which he promotes *The Bondman*—their insistance, and their establishment of a spurious tempo.

I have suggested that Heinemann's publishing practices overdetermined the combination of romance and realism which Caine strives for in *The Bondman*. Caine himself avowed that combination as his artistic purpose in a lecture in Edinburgh in 1894; the trend in the novel, he said then, was toward the "realistic romance":

> May I, without irreverence, say that I dream of a greater novel than we have yet seen—a novel that shall be a compound of the plain nineteenth century realism of the penny newspaper and the pure and lofty idealism of the Sermon on the Mount—the plainest realism and the highest idealism?

The *Saturday Review*, specialists in irreverence ("let the reeling imagination try to grasp the notion of such a compound"), would grant only that Hall Caine had so far attained half of his ideal, "the 'realism,' let us say (or is it the 'idealism'?) of the *Daily Telegraph*."[37] But given the devices Caine used to structure his novels, the average *Daily Telegraph* reader might well have had difficulty distinguishing in them the "realism" from the "romance." Caine selected familiar biblical themes:

> When I began to think of a theme, I found four or five subjects clamouring for a acceptance. There was the story of the Prodigal Son, which afterwards became "The Deemster"; the story of Jacob and Esau, which in the same way turned into "The Bondman"; the story of Samuel and Eli, which after a fashion moulded itself finally into "The Scapegoat.". . .[38]

This was the main device by which Caine sought to mediate realism and romance for a popular audience, at the same time forestalling, in the same audience, fears of impurity.

The Bondman is set in Iceland, where Stephen Orry, a powerful, dissolute man, deserts his wife, daughter of the governor-general of the

island, and sails to the Isle of Man, where he marries again and has
a son, Michael. The first wife, meanwhile, has also borne a son, Jason,
and on her deathbed, nineteen years later, she orders him to avenge
her and to kill Stephen and Michael. But on the Isle of Man Stephen
Orry has repented and he sends Michael to Iceland to arrange a reconciliation. Michael, of course, cannot now do this, but he stays in Iceland,
prospers, and is elected president when Iceland successfully rebels
against Danish rule. In the meantime, Jason, having come to Man on
his mission of revenge, unwittingly saves his father from drowning,
though Stephen then dies in Jason's arms. Jason falls in love with the
daughter of Adam Fairbrother, deputy governor of the Isle of Man,
Greeba, who is engaged to Michael and is awaiting his return from
Iceland. Greeba goes to Iceland and marries Michael, with Jason following. In Iceland, the two brothers each commit acts against the state
and, sworn enemies but still not knowing each other's identity, find
themselves chained together in the sulfur mines. During this ordeal
Jason becomes Michael's devoted friend and eventually dies for him.
These tortuous details, Hall Caine's reworking of the Jacob/Esau story,
trace the novel's ideological determinations.

Frederic Whyte suggests that *The Bondman* "came out at the right
hour," the hour of what was being called by contemporary critics "local
fiction"; Quiller-Couch, for example, places Caine with "Mr Barrie
in the north," "Mr Hardy in the south," but also with "Mr Hornung
in Australia" and "Mr Kipling scouring the wide world, but returning
always to India." [39] The names Kipling and Hornung give "local" an
odd twist; what "Q" and Whyte are getting at is less the "local" than
"the wide world," the diverse localities which, however much like home,
are to a metropolitan reader socially, culturally, and sometimes politically *foreign*. The "hour" of these writers, and of *The Bondman*, is historically an example of what we have discussed in Chapter 3, the
material restructuring of the local and foreign in the interest of modern
publishing capital. *The Bondman* makes a romance of this experience
of difference. For *The Bondman* is, in Stevenson's phrase, "a novel of
circumstance," in which, as the *Times* reviewer put it, while "the author
has strained chronology to his purpose," [40] the Jacob/Esau relation produces "realistically" a series of coincidental "situations." The imprison-
ment in the sulfur mine is just one of many examples: others include
Stephen Orry's shipwreck and rescue ("the moment when the watch
had been changed had been the very moment when Stephen Orry had

run down the flare"),[41] Michael's presidency of Iceland ("violating more than one regulation touching my age, nationality and period of residence in Iceland" [2:96]), and Adam Fairbrother's encounter in Iceland with the captive Michael (" 'Lord-a-massy, who's this,' cried Jack" [3:29]). As the *Times* reviewer remarked, "the story is barbarously over-crowded with incident and tempestuous passion," and the coincidences are merely one kind of deliberate, progressive articulation of incident. The *Westminster* reviewer, welcoming the new novelist in 1887, was not bothered by Caine's reliance on coincidence: "in what, it may fairly be asked, does the function of the romance consist, if every avenue of the merely improbable is to be rigidly forbidden its followers?"[42] The tempo of this awkward progression of "incidents" quickens as the novel approaches its "epic" climax. Chapter 12 of book 2 is unusually divided into short numbered sections which trace the ins and outs of the conspiracy of Greeba's brothers against Michael, and again in book 3 this abrupt juxtaposition of incident serves as a jerky sort of plot mechanism, ignoring "realistic" causality "that we may stride on faster" (3:122).

Reviewers made much of Hall Caine's style. The *Academy* found that, despite "some truant angularity," "the language of *The Bondman* is full of nervous, graphic, and poetical English." The poetical English mostly exhibits that quality which the *Times* found in Caine's characterization, "a semi-Scriptural primitiveness,"[43] characterized syntactically by inversions, by sentences beginning with adverbial phrases and with "and" and "but," as well as by biblical diction, as in the birth of Jason at the beginning of chapter 3:

> Of Rachel in her dishonour there is now not much to tell, but the little that is left is the kernel of this history.
> That night, amid the strain of strong emotions, she was brought to bed before her time was yet full. Her labour was hard, and long she lay between life and death, for the angel of hope did not pull with her. (1:31)

This sort of "poeticality" not only signals a romance of incident and situation, a "romantic realism," but guarantees its suitability to the widest audience. For if the preconstructed discourse of *The Bondman* might be said to depend on the Bible, its transverse discourse, its earnest attempt to go beyond the preconstructed, is a sentimentalized representation of the position of women and the softer, "feminine" virtues in a world of patriarchal anger and brutality: "this story of how two good men with a good woman between them pursued each other over the earth with vows of vengeance, and came together at length in Heaven's good time and way" (3:1). Greeba, the woman between, moves through the story within an ideological field of marital duty/romantic love:wifely affection/adultery. The novel nowhere imagines any sharper contrast to romantic love than what I have termed "wifely affection," and this lacuna produces that sentimentality which is (with "firmness") patriarchal capitalism's characteristic emotion. Deeply implicated in the rivalry between the brothers, Greeba must be the agent of their climactic reconciliation. When Jason carries Michael into the midst of the Althing, the ancient Icelandic assembly on the Mount of Laws, the sobbing Greeba throws herself on the insensible Michael, and Jason, at last realizing their relationship, renounces vengeance: "One look at the piteous blind face lying on Greeba's bosom, one glance at the more piteous wet face that hung over it, and love had conquered hate in that big heart for ever and for ever" (3:158–59).

What determine the language of this scene and its dramatic place in *The Bondman* are the necessities of the patriarchal/capitalist literary mode of production, mediated through Heinemann's entrepreneurial publishing practices and ideologies of gender. Stephen Orry's wronged Icelandic wife and his sluttish Manx wife present types which illuminate Greeba's difference, as the type of sentimental wifely affection. This transverse discourse overlays the biblical tale of vengeful brothers so as to make the novel "fresh" and "to the moment," just as the setting, or the combined Icelandic/Manx settings, catch the very "hour," world-wide, of the "local, yet foreign." And all these elements of textual ideology enact that overlapping of "realism" and "romance" in the popular ideology of the early nineties, gratifying as well the economic purposes and artistic pretensions of a popular, entrepreneurial publisher in the emerging literary mode of production. I want now to measure these hypotheses against a slightly later work, by a female writer, from another publisher.

2. In late 1884, Mary Mackay, the daughter of Dr. Charles Mackay, a journalist and minor literary figure, sent four sonnets on Shake-spearean themes to George Bentley, the head of Richard Bentley and Son, publishers of *Temple Bar*, a shilling monthly for "the comfortable, literate, but ill-educated middle class."[44] Her father enclosed a letter,

introducing "Miss Marie Corelli" to Bentley, who, while he did not publish the sonnets, encouraged her and invited further submissions, and in July 1885 *Temple Bar* published Marie Corelli's essay "One of the World's Wonders."[45] Further encouraged, Marie Corelli wrote her first novel, which she called "Lifted Up" and sent to Bentley in late 1885. Bentley's readers, one of whom was Hall Caine, wrote "violently opposed," "vitriolic" reports on the manuscript, but Bentley judged it otherwise, writing to Marie Corelli that "the book, as a story, is bold, clever, extravagant; it is an effort of wild imagination."[46] He offered her, according to differing accounts, £40 on publication, with a further £30 at 600 copies and £30 on 750 copies.[47] A strange science-fiction fantasy about (literally) "personal electricity," the novel was published in two volumes at 21s. as *A Romance of Two Worlds* in February 1886. It was barely noticed in the *Pall Mall Gazette*, and reviewed harshly in the *Globe*, *World*, and *Whitehall Review*, but treated more kindly, if guardedly, by the *Athenaeum*: "The book will make no converts; but considered as a romance, pure and simple, it may entertain its readers not a little."[48] But *A Romance of Two Worlds* was a popular success— "Marie Corelli had in fact achieved the writer's dream of capturing the loyalty of a public in spite of adverse critical opinion"[49]—and she brought out a second novel in the late summer of 1886, *Vendetta*, which paid her "rather more than she had received for the *Romance*—£50 on publication and a further £50 if sales reached 550 copies."[50] *Vendetta* was reviewed slightly more favorably, but again the novel was a popular success; a second edition was announced on 9 October, "and on October 22, Mr Bentley sent a substantial royalty cheque," with "very great pleasure because I should have been mortified beyond expression if the public had not responded to the marked power of your story."[51]

Over the next five years, Marie Corelli published with Bentley *Thelma* (3 vols., 1887), *Ardath* (3 vols., 1887), *Wormwood* (3 vols., 1890), and *The Soul of Lilith* (3 vols., 1892). For *The Soul of Lilith* she received £250 upon signing the contract, £250 on publication, and a royalty of 6s. a copy after the first 1,500 sold.[52] Bentley was a cautious publisher, Royal Gettmann writes, hardly what we have seen as "entrepreneurial":

> In fiction George Bentley valued entertainment and story-telling, and he was apprehensive of whatever was extravagant or thoroughly original in choice of subject matter or treatment. His novelists might

touch upon the slightly daring, but never in such a way as to threaten the innocence of the Young Thing.[53]

Marie Corelli shared some of these values, but she also had some "extravagant" practices. Her biographers emphasize her complex, neurotic personality and her unusual personal life, but the brutality of reviewers toward her, and her position as a woman writer overdetermined whatever psychological tensions she endured. In 1892 she published anonymously with another publisher, Lamley, a "satire" of contemporary public figures—reviewers, competitors for popularity such as Kipling, and politicians, including Gladstone, who had paid her a visit in 1889 to compliment her on *Ardath*. Unfortunately, she also disparaged Bentley, his firm, and even his house in Slough, and after 1893 Marie Corelli's connection with Bentley was ended.[54] In early October of that year she published with Methuen *Barabbas*, a novel about the crucifixion and resurrection of Christ, in three volumes. At the same time that Bentley was selling her earlier novels in its "Favourite Novels" series, an extension of the "Standard Novels" idea which had introduced "Bentleyism" (6s. novels in small 8vo format which assumed that "contemporary novels could aspire to the epithet 'standard' "),[55] Methuen was announcing (8 November) that the large first edition of *Barabbas* was "exhausted," and on 2 December that the third edition was "in the press."[56] Methuen was another of the "new imprints" in British publishing of the late eighties, having begun as publishers "appropriately," says Eileen Duffy, "with a still-born whiff of theology, and with fiction." Mumby and Norrie write:

> From its earliest days the Methuen list was a splendid amalgam of fiction, non-fiction and academic works, catering for all brows, but with an eye to building a healthy back list.

Their first two novels were by the Rev. Sabine Baring Gould, the composer of "Onward Christian Soldiers," and Edna Lyall. Edna Lyall's novel *Derrick Vaughan, Novelist* also initiated "Methuen's long association with and reliance on the work of writers who were women, many of whom have been and are concerned with what in the 1890s was known as the 'woman question' and is now called feminism."[57]

    I shall want to examine more closely Marie Corelli's contradictory insertion into the Woman Question, but here I might simply note details of her writer's business practice which invite such an examination. Marie Corelli employed no literary agent in her relations either with Bentley or with Methuen. She wrote in the *Idler* in 1893 that "authors, like other people, should learn how to manage their own affairs themselves,"

> that when they take a paid agent into their confidence, they make
> an open confession of their business incapacity, and voluntarily elect
> to remain in foolish ignorance of the practical part of their profession.

Unspoken, of course, is that "business incapacity" was conventionally taken to characterize women. Elsewhere in this essay Marie Corelli denies that she is "a 'strong-minded' woman, with egotistical ideas of a 'mission,'" claiming to be only a "literary woman, . . . fighting a hard fight."[58] As Arnold Bennett was to remark, "she must tilt or she will die,"[59] and she would appear indeed to have fought a hard fight with her publishers—she was "case-hardened," said Methuen.[60] She was "the most troublesome of [Bentley's] writers," according to Royal Gettmann, who describes an agreement with Bentley which would appear to have given her a far more favorable percentage of the profits from the cheap edition of *Thelma* than Rhoda Broughton had been able to obtain from Bentley for one of her novels.[61] Marie Corelli's letters to Bentley press him on all aspects of the novels' production, from advertising to the arrangements for foreign and colonial copyright; indeed, one cause of their breakup was her demanding an independent audit of their account.[62] Her most "extravagant" innovation, one which Bentley would not have tolerated but which Methuen allowed, was to insert at the head of page 1 of *The Sorrows of Satan*, the novel which followed *Barabbas*, a "SPECIAL NOTICE" to reviewers:

> No Copies of this Book are sent out for review. Members of the Press
> will therefore obtain it (should they wish to do so) in the usual way
> with the rest of the public, i.e., through the Booksellers and Libraries.[63]

But the tension itself, between what Marie Corelli denies ("a strong-minded woman") and what she claims ("a literary woman"), is ideologically the most significant point, representing not only the ambiguity of her self-dramatization but a crucial element of textual ideology in her next novel.

The Sorrows of Satan was published on 21 October 1895. On 5 October, the *Pall Mall Gazette* had speculated on the import of its announced title, adopting the patriarchal tone that the journals were so often to use toward Marie Corelli's work:

> We do not exactly gather to what period of a tolerably protracted career she will lend fresh and ultra-Satanic interest; but the fall from Paradise readily suggests itself. The fact that old out-of-date Milton has already dealt with the subject need not trouble a lady who has written up the Crucifixion. "Things unattempted yet in prose or rhyme," he called his effusion. Dear simple old soul![64]

The Sorrows of Satan is in fact a story of Satan's activities in the worlds of publishing and upper-class society in contemporary England. Subtitled "The Strange Experience of One Geoffrey Tempest, Millionaire," it tells how Tempest, struggling to publish his first novel, suddenly inherits £5 million from a distant relative in South America, at the same time that an Oxford acquaintance now in Australia writes to him to introduce a wealthy, handsome, and sophisticated friend, Lucio Rimânez. As several reviewers were quick to point out, this is Lucifer Ahrimanes, who, as Lucio, becomes Tempest's closest friend and advisor. Tempest is immediately introduced by Lucio into fashionable (what Marie Corelli calls "swagger") society and encounters its population of rich wastrels, while at the same time, by publishing his novel at his own expense and allowing his publisher to "boom" it, he becomes a famous author. Lucio arranges for Tempest to marry Lady Sibyl Elton, the beautiful but cynically depraved daughter of a bankrupt peer. Their lavish wedding festivities, which Lucio arranges at Tempest's country-house, allow Marie Corelli to satirize upper-class life; indeed, the novel attacks "swagger society" again and again. Soon after her wedding Lady Sibyl attempts to seduce Lucio, who rejects her, and Tempest abandons her, only to return when she commits suicide, leaving a two-chapter-long, autobiographical suicide note. Tempest then leaves England on Lucio's yacht and travels to Egypt where Lucio reveals his true identity. In a fantastic episode Lucio/Lucifer demands Tempest's allegiance. Tempest instead chooses God and is abandoned by Lucio in mid-Atlantic where he is rescued by a steamer bound for England. He loses his fortune and begins a new life, perhaps with Mavis Clare, a neighbor of Tempest's and a popular novelist. Mavis Clare has been presented as gentle and good, and able to resist the devilish seductions which ruin the others. Also, as W. T. Stead and other reviewers pointed out, in her description and in her presentation of herself, Mavis Clare seems remarkably like Marie Corelli.[65] The textual ideology of this melodrama, which had an immediate sale greater than that of any previous English novel,[66] is historically significant, but I would like first to discuss the circumstances of its production.

Methuen advertised *Barabbas*, now in a popular edition, through the spring and summer of 1895, and it had reached an eighteenth edition by 21 September. Its first edition had been "large," and according to Michael Sadleir it was her first book to achieve "a popularity of inescapable significance." Methuen's advertisement in the *Athenaeum* for 5 October makes it clear that the first three editions, all in three volumes, were sold out in the first six months, with the next seven one-volume editions being exhausted over the next six months.[67] The earliest public mention of *The Sorrows of Satan* that I have found was the 5 October *Pall Mall Gazette*'s advice on the treatment of Satan, followed by a brief mention in the "Notes about Books" column of the *Clarion*, the socialist weekly, for 12 October. Methuen announced in the *Pall Mall Gazette* for 18 October (i.e., *before* its publication) that "the very large first edition of this book being considerably oversubscribed a second edition is in the press." Refining the practice adopted by publishers like Heinemann when their three-volume novels were republished in one volume, Methuen's advertisements in the *Guardian* and *Pall Mall Gazette* during the first week of publication proclaimed that the first edition of 15,000 copies, and a second edition of 5,000, had been exhausted before publication, and a third edition of 5,000 copies was in the press.[68] Advertisements in the *Athenaeum* and the *Saturday Review* on 2 November then stated that the third edition was nearly exhausted; by 30 November, a seventh edition was in the press, and by 14 December, a ninth edition.[69] *The Sorrows of Satan* had sold out its first three editions, 25,000 copies at 6s., in a week; *Barabbas*, in three volumes at 31s. 6d., had taken six weeks for the same number of (indeterminate) editions. Eight editions of *The Sorrows of Satan*, presumably 50,000 copies, were sold in its first seven weeks; *Barabbas* had needed eight months for that number of editions, and W. T. Stead claimed that *The Sorrows of Satan* sold "some seventy thousand copies" by the end of 1895.[70] Clearly Methuen's exploitation of the new cheap format and their advertising in the daily and weekly press, broadcasting almost weekly the rate at which the novel was selling, were determinate factors in producing the "hysterical triumph" [71] of Marie Corelli's first one-volume novel.

But these factors are, of course, massively overdetermined by the text. And the "text" which Methuen were able to sell so widely was not simply the published text of *The Sorrows of Satan*, although it was that also. While Stead, in the *Review of Reviews*, might see the novelist's self-portraiture, as Mavis Clare, as "touching," that self-portrait merely makes explicit the extent to which the commodity-text, *The Sorrows of Satan*, included "Marie Corelli." Marie Corelli's denials that she would be "so *conceited* as to draw *my own picture* in that ideal conception" to the contrary,[72] "Mavis Clare" is the extreme instance of her self-promotion. W. L. Courtney, in the *Daily Telegraph*, regretted that the novel's critical asides "give a somewhat unpleasant personal note to what should have been the working out of a large and impersonal theme." [73] Her various biographies assign different meanings to this intrusion of personality but give copious examples besides "Mavis Clare": George Bullock calls attention to the charges of self-advertisement arising from her decision to withold review copies of *The Sorrows of Satan* and suggests that "most of her heroines, even though she was not aware of it, were expressions of the perfect state of spiritual development to which she believed herself to have attained." Speaking of her attempts to conceal her private history, he says that "she made quite certain that only a conventional aspect was given to the public." Eileen Bigland writes that Marie Corelli was "the show-piece among the eccentrics. . . . At any sort of function she could be relied upon to create a sensation," and Brian Masters mentions the gossip she was able to create, pointing, like the other biographers, to how she exploited her meetings with Gladstone and the Prince of Wales.[74] Her essay "My First Book" in the *Idler*, illustrated with photographs of "Villa Occupied by Miss Marie Corelli on the Lake of Geneva," "Miss Corelli's House in Kensington (Back View)," and so on, is determinedly personal in the manner of the "new journalism," as she attempts to come "straight into close and sympathetic union with my public." [75] In these ways (a process with which we have since become very familiar) a "Marie Corelli" was created which was a determinate element of the "text" of her best-seller, a constituent feature of a new, direct distribution of text, unmediated by reviewers and lending libraries.[76] As one of her admirers wrote, Marie Corelli "is suburban and the delight of Suburbia"; "she is the idol of Suburbia—the favourite of the common multitude." [77] The Victorian suburb was not only "the seat of respectability," but "a world of fantasy in which dreams of self-importance and fulfillment could become tangible in the management of some doll's house estate and in the occupation of a unique social niche." The Victorian suburbs, like *The Sorrows of Satan*, were "the objects of ridicule and even contempt," and the expanded, "Marie Corelli" text of *The Sorrows of Satan*, again like "suburbia," was "the product of a whole social and economic process set in motion by a curious blend of romantic idealism and hard-headed realism." [78]

But the ideology of the printed text *The Sorrows of Satan* does not lie simply in its representation of London society, the literary world, or the suburban ethos. Marie Corelli's critics attacked her for her "vulgarities," her ignorance, for example, of the plural of *arpeggio*, for spelling "Sybil," "Sibyl," or for her faults of expression, as in Tempest and Lucio's "lotus-like voyage up the Nile" (443). Much of this criticism, as in Stead's charge of "shrewish spitefulness" or the *Pall Mall Gazette*'s patronizing "a lady who has written up the Crucifixion," readily betrays its patriarchal assumptions. Marie Corelli indeed does not portray well the male world of Oxford—"we were brimful of Homer and the thoughts and maxims of all the immortal Greeks and Latins" (8)—but the reviewers' comments on her use of "swagger" again imply exactly a patriarchal/class judgment. [79] *The Sorrows of Satan* is a collection of stock literary devices and situations, from Lucio's gothic moments (see 40, 238–39) to Sibyl's situation as a bartered bride. But these, as well as the novel's attacks on reviewers and critics like Andrew Lang ("McWhing" [100]), displeased only her more sophisticated readers. The novel's presentment of ideologies of gender, and its construction of "Mavis Clare" as we have seen, were challenging yet comfortable. The idea of the *male* which the novel presents is almost wholly conventional, but Corelli attempts to portray Geoffrey Tempest as one who moves beyond that position under the influence of "Mavis Clare." At the beginning Tempest loftily considers that women "were created to amuse men,—not to instruct them" (139). When he meets Sibyl, the "danger-flash" in her eyes, "the delicate quiver of pride," and the "warm flush of indignation" all suggest spirit and untamed will, "and rouses in a man the love of mastery that is born in his nature, urging him to conquer and subdue that which seems unconquerable" (144). More particularly, Tempest says, "I hate women who write" (183), and he shares the conventional view of women novelists as " 'unsexed females' and repulsive blue-stockings" (230).

The novel's most significant preoccupation ideologically is with
contemporary popular ideologies of the "new": the "new fiction," the
"new poets," and most important, the "new woman." Sibyl reveals in
her suicide epistle that she was first corrupted, as a young girl, by a
"horrible, lascivious" novel by a woman:

> I had seen it praised in all the leading journals of the day; its
> obscenities were hinted as "daring,"—its vulgarities were quoted as
> "brilliant wit,"—in fact so many laudatory columns were written
> about it in the press that I resolved to read it again. Encouraged by
> the "literary censors" of the time, I did so, and little by little the
> insidious abomination of it filtered into my mind and *stayed there.*
> (405)

Then an acquaintance, the daughter of a marchioness, introduced this
Young Person to Swinburne's poetry and she achieved "a complete
knowledge of things evil and pernicious" (408). Before their marriage
she amazes Tempest with her "bit of Ibsenism, or whatever other ism
affects me" (205), revealing that, "thanks to newspapers, magazines and
'decadent' novels . . . there is nothing in the rôle of marriage that I do
not know, though I am not yet twenty" (204). Later she scornfully
justifies to Tempest her attempt to seduce Lucio by reference to "the
'new' fiction":

> Your ideas of domestic virtue are quite out of date. Both men and
> women are, according to accepted writers of the day, at equal liberty
> to love when they will, and where they may. Polygamous purity is
> the "new" creed! Such love, in fact, so we are taught, constitutes the
> only "sacred" union. If you want to alter this "movement," and
> return to the old-fashioned types of the modest maiden and the im-
> maculate matron, you must sentence all the "new" writers of prof-
> itable pruriency to penal servitude for life, and institute a Govern-
> ment censorship of the modern press. (371–72)

The Sorrows of Satan locates the source of "decadent" novels (indeed,
as one publishers tells Geoffrey Tempest, of books "on any positively
indecent subject") in "the 'New' woman" (6), the object of Marie
Corelli's most persistent attack. Even Satan, as Lucio, is appalled by
the "number of females clamouring like unnatural hens in a barn-yard
about their 'rights' and 'wrongs' " (386). Presumably finding some profit

itself in occasional pruriency, *The Sorrows of Satan* yet attempts in its presentment of Mavis Clare an alternative to both "the new creed" and the "old-fashioned types."

While on its manifest level *The Sorrows of Satan* draws on the conventional contraries, the virgin and the whore, it attempts on a latent level to achieve an understanding of the New Woman of the eighties and nineties. This understanding is not very profound, as it simply rings the changes on popular images of the New Woman as rebellious, promiscuous, and noisily proselytizing. *The Sorrows of Satan* cannot admit what Gail Cunningham has convincingly argued is an essential characteristic of the genuine "New Woman": "a woman was only genuinely New if her conflict with social convention was on *a matter of principle*." [80] The New Woman of *The Sorrows of Satan* is unprincipled, has no essential characteristic beyond her posturing. The principle, of course, is found in the novel's implied contrary ideological position, its genuinely "New" woman, neither angel, nor wanton, nor clamoring suffragette, "Mavis Clare," whose distinctive, redemptive characteristic would seem to be "independence." As an artist, Mavis Clare, for instance, is independent of malicious criticism: "I am certain that calumny and misrepresentation, though it may move me to compassion cannot disturb my peace" (229). Her peaceful independence puts forward a compromise conservative ideological position. Recognizing, indeed dramatizing, the dangers to the Young Person of candor in fiction, *The Sorrows of Satan* nevertheless rejects the old-fashioned types of the modest maiden and the immaculate matron. Instead it presents Mavis Clare as a different and better ideal: intellectual, independent, at peace, and "more than a match for the publishers all round" (142). Reflecting in this way "the ambiguous or negative attitudes of many of her readers," [81] "Mavis Clare" combines with the public persona "Marie Corelli" to produce a crucial component of a commodity-text which, as the *Literary Year-Book* commented in 1897, "is read alike in palaces and omnibuses." [82] W. T. Stead said of *The Sorrows of Satan*:

> Let no one despise it. It is the supreme example of a popular style; the zenith attained by the Penny Dreadfulesque in the last decade of the nineteenth century. [83]

A materialist historian would agree that it need not be despised, but would add that it reached that zenith only through the combined entrepreneurial efforts of Marie Corelli and Methuen, within the new patriarchal/capitalist literary mode of production.

3. In January 1897, Arnold Bennett, whose own first novel was soon to be published by John Lane's Bodley Head, reviewed the theatrical version of *The Sorrows of Satan* for *Woman*, a penny weekly which he edited. Bennett dismissed the "prodigious, Titanic absurdity" of the play, but, while patronizing its author in the style of the *Saturday Review* or *Pall Mall Gazette*, he was slightly more tolerant of the novel: "I, at any rate, have read it. . . . I enjoyed it. I found it amusing, and even grammatical. Perhaps I found it more amusing than its author intended." [84] Six months later, again in *Woman* and writing as a woman, Bennett composed a facetious "discovery" of the works of Marie Corelli, mocking her private/public life, the settings of her novels, her "truly original style," and her moral seriousness: "none, I make bold to say, is more worthy to carry on the work of Thomas Carlyle as a scourge and lash of our social system." The breathless "feminine" critic ended: "My bookseller told me that *The Sorrows of Satan* is Miss Corelli's best work. So I am reading it. Satan is perfectly *sweet*." [85] Bennett's review of Marie Corelli's *The Master-Christian* in the *Academy* in 1897 again dismissed the novel as "absurd past all telling," while admiring to a degree the fact that "her inventive faculty has always ranged easily and unafraid amid the largest things." For, as Bennett said, "there is not a writer living today who does not envy Miss Corelli her circulation." [86] Assistant editor of *Woman* in 1894, Bennett, as "Barbara," wrote a weekly column, "Book Chat," and in August of that year he reviewed Hall Caine's latest novel, *The Manxman*. *The Bondman* and *The Scapegoat*, he wrote, "were good, perhaps fine, but surely not the colossal works of genius which all the newspapers of the kingdom and a certain statesman [Gladstone] would have us believe." *The Manxman*, on the other hand, was "a work of high genius . . . unsurpassed in modern fiction." "To speak plainly," he wrote, *The Manxman* was "perfect." [87] By 1897, Bennett had tempered his admiration for Hall Caine's work. *The Christian*, published that year, was "the worst novel that Mr Hall Caine has yet written." Bennett censured *The Christian*'s shallowness, its fatigued stock figures, and the triteness of its plot, as well as objecting to Caine's carrying the "uses of advertisements a little too far" by publishing private letters, including one from Gladstone, applauding the book. A natural comparison suggested itself: "It is better than Marie Corelli but not much better: it belongs to the same crowd

as *The Sorrows of Satan.*"[88] The young Arnold Bennett, on the verge of publishing his first novel, was clearly learning from the example of both Hall Caine and Marie Corelli how to publish in what he called in the *Academy* "a market gloriously dazzling to the commercial instinct."[89] He saw clearly the value of such an entrepreneurial instinct; as "Jacob Tonson" in the *New Age* in 1908 he was to recall one of its innovations:

> It was the commercial genius of Mr Hall Caine that invented the idea of publishing important novels during the "off" season [August/September]. Miss Marie Corelli, by a sure instinct, followed suit. And now all sorts of stars, from genuine artists to mere successful artisans, take care to publish in the off season.[90]

By 1897 Arnold Bennett was certainly a successful artisan. Before he came to London from the Potteries he had been an occasional journalist for the *Staffordshire Knot* and the *Sentinel,* and after 1889, as a solicitor's clerk in London, he won a *Tit-Bits* parody competition and published articles and short stories in the evening papers the *Sun* and the *Star.* In 1893, he was appointed assistant editor of *Woman,* becoming editor in 1896 and remaining there until he decided in 1900 to support himself by his writing.[91] *Woman,* founded in 1887, was aimed at the educated woman; its motto, on the cover of every issue, was "Forward! But Not Too Fast." It offered "something more than the 'Lady's,' or 'Society' paper or cookery book, and something less than the ponderous daily leader and parliamentary reports, or the academic weekly or monthly review."[92] During these early years as well, Bennett developed an interest in rare books; a friend in the solicitor's office "taught me to regard a book, not as an instrument for obtaining information or emotion, but as a *book,* printed at such a place in such a year by so-and-so, bound by so-and-so, and carrying colophons, registers, water-marks, and *fautes d'impression.*"[93] As we have seen, in the late 1880s and early 1890s there was "something approaching a craze for first editions," and Bennett and his fellow clerk issued in 1891 and 1892 two volumes of an uncompleted catalogue of bibliographical rarities. And as the increasing contemporary interest in rare books was one of the determining factors in Elkin Mathews and John Lane's founding of the "Bodley Head," it is no surprise that in 1893–94 Bennett, when his short story "A Letter Home" was rejected by a popular weekly, should send it to the *Yellow Book*, which was, in a sense, a house journal for the Bodley Head.[94] But before discussing the Bodley Head I want to examine more closely Arnold Bennett's early journalism.

James Hepburn, Bennett's editor, addresses the charge against Bennett of "pot-boiling" and concludes generously that Bennett "could hardly help boiling the pot fast and furiously." He lists the range of papers, from the *Academy* to the *Sun*, which eventually invited Bennett's work and argues that he had "a natural gift for popular writing," popular "in the sense of mass appeal" and "according to the sort of audience it met."[95] It is significant, however, that, at least until 1900, Bennett never published in any of the "principal monthlies and quarterlies" surveyed by the *Wellesley Index*, the forty-three "journals of relatively high calibre in the writing and editing, and of considerable reputation in educated circles."[96] This choice, or exclusion, sharpens the questions of sorts of audience, mass appeal, and Bennett's "natural gift." For, as we have seen, he had a gift also for perceiving audiences as markets, recognizing similar perceptions in Hall Caine and Marie Corelli. When he decided on "the vocation of letters," he says in *The Truth about an Author*, he chose "not scholarship, not the dilettantism of belles-lettres, but sheer constructive journalism and possibly fiction."[97] "Constructive journalism" seems to be Bennett's name for accepting capitalist relations of production in writing, along with the sort of empirical analysis of those relations which would allow the journalist not only to cope but to prosper. Not only did Bennett record in his *Journal*, for instance, the current "prices per thousand" given different writers by Tillotson's Fiction Bureau,[98] but his various books of vocational advice over the years generalized this sort of positivist knowledge and his own experience as a writer. *How to Become an Author* (1903), for example, derived its "divisions of literature" from a survey of the kinds of new books published in 1902. Because there are more writers engaged in fiction, and novelists have more "esteem, influence, renown and notoriety," he dealt exclusively with fiction, beginning with journalism because "it is a fact that very many, if not most, authors begin by being journalists." Focusing then on the "literary" (as opposed to the "mechanical") branch of journalism, he demonstrated by comparing rates of pay how the journalist "sells his brains in a weak market."[99] In *The Truth about an Author* (1901), Bennett described his own practice:

> As a journeyman author, with the ability and inclination to turn my
> pen in any direction at request, I long ago established a rule never
> to work for less than ten shillings an hour on piece-work. . . . But
> each year I raise my price per hour. Of course, when I am working
> on my own initiative, for the sole advancement of my artistic reputa-
> tion, I ignore finance and think of glory alone. It cannot, however,
> be too clearly understood that the professional author . . . is eternally
> compromising between glory and something more edible and
> warmer at nights.[100]

In 1904 Bennett was to tell his agent, J. B. Pinker, "You don't yet realise
what an engine for the production of fiction you have in me,"[101] but
far from being an accident or a "natural gift," that engine had itself
been produced by the relations of novel production and by Bennett's
knowing adaptation to those relations. When he said, in 1898, that
he proposed for the next year "to give myself absolutely to writing the
sort of fiction that sells itself,"[102] his emphasis was on "sells," for he
had studied every detail of salesmanship. His submitting "A Letter
Home" to the *Yellow Book* in 1894 had been determined both by that
knowledge and by publishing relations.

The Bodley Head, as I have mentioned, appeared as a publisher's
imprint amidst the increased interest in antiquarian books at the end
of the eighties and the "revival of printing" which accompanied the
founding of William Morris' Kelmscott Press in 1891 and the work of
the book designers Walter Blaikie, Charles Jacobi, and Charles Ricketts.
Elkin Mathews was an "Ancient and Modern Bookseller" in Exeter
when John Lane suggested that he join him in London to establish a
firm dedicated to excellence in book production. "The Bodley Head
book" very quickly came to be recognized for its "beauty and aura of
high quality." James Nelson describes it as "simply beautiful, achieving in its format an aesthetic appeal derived oftentimes from the taste-
ful arrangement of the most economical materials."[103] R. D. Brown
has shown the economics of the Bodley Head book in detail, how
Mathews and Lane regularly employed large type sizes and large leadings
to cut compositor's costs, and used remainders of fine papers to produce small numbers of slim volumes which were then inexpensive to
bind. As Brown says of the Bodley Head aim to present "the freshest
and most daring of the 'new' poets in limited editions that were inexpensive but nevertheless exquisite examples of the art of fine book-

making," the physical character of these editions was dictated by "the means at the disposal of the press."[104] John Lane "saw himself as a specialist publisher to the cognoscenti, issuing carefully selected books in carefully produced and always limited editions." The early Bodley Head books, then, were conceived of as art objects, "beautiful and rare examples of fine bookmaking which might someday be valuable as first editions."[105] Although the early Bodley Head almost totally ignored fiction, when the partnership broke up in September 1894 and Mathews continued producing choice volumes of belles lettres, Lane, taking with him the Bodley Head imprint, turned to "quality books of a generally popular variety." J. E. Morpungo suggests that Lane had come to be recognized as the more enterprising of the two partners, but that, after the separation, John Lane's Bodley Head declined with his move from limited editions into competition with "well-established general houses with healthier finances."[106]

The *Yellow Book* was first published in April 1894, and two issues appeared before Mathews and Lane ended their partnership. A 5s. quarterly, it was "a typically 'luxury at low cost' Bodley Head item."[107] It was, for instance, typographically different from its competitors. Printed in Caslon old-face type, it was composed on linotype machines, although it used catchwords to give the impression that it had been hand set. The *Yellow Book* had a booklike format and "the majesty of quarterly publication." Its pages were uncut, and with its soft, rag-content (if machine-made) paper it was "a speculation with slender risk and expectation of fat profit." Lane knew how to create and exploit literary fashions:

> What Lane intended to profit from was the need of the *avant garde* to advance from the safe world of the coterie to the dangerous open world of the "new," and the complementary need of the popular press—the "new" journalism—to find (or if necessary engineer) controversy. The position of the "advanced" and the "new" could be vulgarized and polarized.[108]

For four issues, the *Yellow Book* pursued this course; with the breakup of the Lane-Mathews partnership in the autumn of 1894, Lane took control of the magazine, just in time to see it implicated in the arrest of Oscar Wilde in April 1895. Volume 5, expected on 15 April, was delayed until 30 April, while Lane had the Beardsley plates for the front cover, title page, and the interior replaced. The general aspect of volume 5 was "restrained," and it opened with William Watson's "Hymn to the Sea"; Watson had been the most eager to purge the *Yellow Book* of Aubrey Beardsley.[109]

Arnold Bennett was not put off by the furor over the *Yellow Book*. In 1893, amidst his early potboiling and book collecting, he had attempted to write "a truly excellent short story," which the *Yellow Book* accepted for publication by November 1894, and Bennett's "A Letter Home" appeared in volume 6, in July 1895.[110] In May 1895, as "Barbara," Bennett had written in *Woman* in support of the *Yellow Book*:

> I like the *Yellow Book*. I emphatically like it; and my regard for it grows in spite of the attitude of the daily Press. . . . I like the *Yellow Book* for its frank and courageous actuality, and because, under all the bludgeonings of cant,
>   Its head is yellow, but unbowed.
> And by "actuality" I must not, of course, be understood to mean the ponderous, topical actuality of the *Review of Reviews*. Far from that! The *Yellow Book* daintily avoids topical subjects, as a cat crossing the street avoids mud. But it is instinct with the inner elusive spirit of the time. It glories in its youth, thereby exhibiting a quality of courage to which few attain. Many have attacked it on the score of affectation, blind to the honest self-expression which underlies its trifling peccadilloes of eccentricity. I would praise it for its eager sincerity. The present volume, the fifth, (John Lane, 5s net), is chiefly remarkable for William Watson's "Hymn to the Sea.". . .[111]

All the ironies, the multiple determinations, of this particular passage need not detain us; I want simply to point out Bennett's decision, in the midst of the Wilde/*Yellow Book* episode, and as his first "excellent" short story moves toward publication in the *Yellow Book*, to endorse (albeit as "Barbara") its "frank and courageous actuality," its "honest self-expression" and "eager sincerity," as elements of "the inner elusive spirit of the time." Here we have an instance of what Hepburn calls Bennett's "first reservations about the creed of realism." [112] Bennett/ "Barbara" is clearly taking a position, not only on the *Yellow Book* and on the longtime issue of decorum, but like the critics we mentioned earlier, he proclaims his commitment to both realism and romance. "A Letter Home," which appeared two months later, does not exhibit the same compromise, but then it had been completed almost two years earlier. Bennett's first novel, *A Man from the North*, however, does exhibit that compromise textual ideology.

Bennett finished writing his novel *A Man from the North* in May 1896 and sent it immediately to the Bodley Head, where it was passed to their young reader, John Buchan, who pronounced it "living" and "convincing." According to *The Truth about an Author*, Lane and Bennett then discussed royalties, Lane offering 5 percent on the first 5,000 copies (of a 3s. 6d. book), and 15 percent thereafter. Hepburn records two discussions: that Lane first offered 5 percent on the first 1,000 copies, 10 percent on the next 1,000, and 15 percent thereafter; the final contract assigns 5 percent to the first 2,000, then 10 percent up to 5,000 copies, and 15 percent thereafter. Bennett acknowledges the irony in their discussing royalties for more than 5,000 copies, but this arrangement was more than what Hepburn calls "academic." [113] Clearly Lane thought the distribution of royalties between 1,000 and 5,000 copies to be worth negotiation: the difference in the two contracts for 2,000 copies is a matter of only £8 15s., but for 5,000 copies, £35 (this compared with the £40 Bentley gave for the first 600 copies of Marie Corelli's first, two-volume novel, with £30 more if he sold 750 copies). John Lane's advertising for *A Man from the North* was restrained, compared with Heinemann's or Methuen's practice. No book was boomed in any fashion in any of the advertisements from 6 November 1897 to 11 June 1898. "John Lane's List" appears in the *Athenaeum* only five weeks during that period, usually as one of three columns on a page. It mentions Bennett's novel as one of six books "now ready" on 5 March (298). On 2 April, it includes a quotation from Eden Philpott's review in *Black and White* (426), removing the quotation on 11 June and listing *A Man from the North* last of the 3s. 6d. novels (771). "John Lane's List" was also published six times in the *Academy* over roughly the same period; there its format was rather more fulsome and the blurb from *Black and White* appeared on 19 March (318). Overall, John Lane's entrepreneurship (or perhaps his operating capital) did not seem to extend to the intense marketing techniques of some of his entrepreneurial colleagues. In *The Truth about an Author*, Bennett claims that his royalties "exceeded the cost of having it typewritten by the sum of one sovereign." [114]

A Man from the North is, first of all, a realist novel. Arnold Bennett, in an essay in the *Academy* in 1901, was to lament the "sameness," "futility," and "lack of enterprise" in the contemporary English novel, that it left fallow the fields which Balzac had tilled.[115] In contrast, his own first novel was written "under the sweet influences of the de Goncourts, Turgenev, Flaubert, and de Maupassant," and he lists in *The Truth about an Author* their "physical characteristics" which he imitated:

> there were to be no poetical quotations in my novel, no titles to the chapters; the narrative was to be divided irregularly into sections by Roman numerals only; and it was indispensable that a certain proportion of these sections should begin or end abruptly.

This describes exactly the physical characteristics of *A Man from the North*, down to the elliptical endings of the sections: "he saw the gleam of appreciative comprehension in their eyes long before his sentences were finished . . ."; "She put her arm gently into his, and pressed it. He had no resistance. . . ."[116] "O succession of dots, charged with significance vague but tremendous," wrote Bennett,

> there were to be hundreds of you in my novel, because you play so important a part in the literature of the country of Victor Hugo and M. Loubet!

But the dots (and the mention of Victor Hugo—Loubet was a Dreyfusard politician) also mark the contradictory impulse toward romance in *A Man from the North*, for Bennett's novel was to be "the Usual miraculously transformed by Art into the Sublime." [117]

Several of the novel's reviewers thought that it had failed in this aim: the *Academy* (for whom Bennett was to become a regular reviewer in four months' time) could detect only "a taste for the elaborate falsehood of M. Zola":

> We conceive that the details have been observed quite accurately, and that they are quite accurately set down, with that absence of passion or palpitation which that kind of story affects, but which makes it singularly dull and wearisome.[118]

The *Athenaeum*, too, found the novel dreary and sordid:

> He supplies, not the poetry of the commonplace, not the romance of the commonplace, but the veriest commonplace of the commonplace.[119]

Bennett's friend, the novelist Eden Philpotts, was not only more kind
but more perceptive (his was the review quoted in John Lane's advertisements). While he acknowledged the realist project of the novel—
the author "permits himself not a word or incident which does not
throw light on character"—Philpotts emphasizes the "inspiration,"
"breadth," and "sympathy": "this artist finds unexpected beauties amid
common things." [120] Philpotts here registers the muted presence in *A
Man from the North* of romance, an impulse Bennett was to acknowledge
more overtly in his journal at this time and over the next few years.
In 1897, on a visit to the north, Bennett went for a walk with his sister
after dark outside Burslem, and he remarked on "the grim and original
beauty of certain aspects of the Potteries":

> Down below is Burslem. . . . It is *not* beautiful in detail, but the
> smoke transforms its ugliness into a beauty transcending the work of
> architects and of time. Though a very old town, it bears no sign of
> great age—the eye is never reminded of its romance and history—but
> instead it thrills and reverberates with the romance of machinery
> and manufacture, the romance of our fight against nature, of the
> gradual taming of the earth's secret forces.

Sixteen months later, his journal records that

> the day of my enthusiasm for "realism," for "naturalism," has passed.
> I can perceive that a modern work of fiction dealing with modern
> life may ignore realism and yet be great. To find beauty, which is
> always hidden—that is the aim.

Three days later, planning a book on modern fiction, Bennett con-
templated a chapter on "the conjuncture of realism with idealism." [121]
And in his three-part *Academy* essay in 1901 entitled "The Fallow Fields
of Fiction," he argued for the "romance" of the London and North
Western main line, or a parish council, or the municipal life of an industrial town, the romance, that is, of "the serious affairs of life." [122]
    A Man from the North is the story of a young man, Richard Larch,
who, like Bennett, comes to London, works as a lawyer's clerk, tries
to write a novel but fails, meets the niece of an older clerk who has
become his friend, fails also in his courtship of the niece, and marries
a cashier in a restaurant. Margaret Drabble writes:

The conclusion is finely realistic: Richard, having lost the superior Adeline, having despaired of his novel, opts for the suburban life, which he knows will prevent him from attempting to write again.

She sees this, indeed the whole novel, as Bennett's "projecting of fears, a confronting of the worst." [123] Bennett himself saw the suburban settings as more central to the novel's conscious artistic project. As "Sarah Volatile," he reviewed the novel himself in *Hearth and Home*, a threepenny women's paper, and there he suggested that the novel's subtitle might have been "The Psychology of the Suburbs," the name of a book planned by Richard Larch and his friend, Richard Aked. [124] Bennett thus underlines his realist intentions in *A Man from the North*, but in calling attention to the "nether greyness" of those suburbs in the ideology of the text, he calls attention also to an emerging romanticist ideology. Aked explains the proposed book to Larch in terms which recall not only Howells and James but Bennett's journal entries:

> the suburbs, even Walham Green and Fulham, are full of interest, for those who can see it. Walk along this very street on such a Sunday afternoon as to-day. The roofs form two horrible, converging straight lines I know, but beneath there is character, individuality, enough to make the greatest book ever written. . . . Even in the thin smoke . . . , the flutter of a blind, the bang of a door, . . . —in all these things there is character and matter of interest—truth waiting to be expounded. (102)

Larch is captivated: "Why . . . had those ideas never presented themselves to *him*? He would write an article on the *character* of Raphael Street" (103). But as he thinks over the planned book, his discourse shifts from realist to romanticist categories:

> Other authors had taken an isolated spot here or there in the suburbs and dissected it, but none had viewed them in their complex entirety; none had attempted to extract from their incoherence a coherent philosophy. (109)

"None" he says, "had suspected that the suburbs were a riddle, the answer to which was not undiscoverable" (110). As Richard looks out of his window the next morning, "all the phenomena of humble life, hitherto witnessed daily without a second thought, now appeared to carry some mysterious meaning which was on the point of declaring itself" (110). While not denying the irony in Bennett's portrayal of Larch, I am struck by the way in which Larch's anticipated epiphany echoes Bennett's own unironical private meditations on "the romance of machinery and manufacture," on "a beauty transcending the work of architects and of time," as "the day of [his] enthusiasm for 'realism' " passes. Thus *A Man from the North*, at the very moment that it antic-ipates the modernist novel, is determined by the ideological struggles of the eighties and nineties; all this, as well, amidst "constructive jour-nalism," and as Bennett prepares "to give myself absolutely to writing the sort of fiction that sells itself," to devote himself entirely to "the cult of the literary *frisson*." [125]

H. G. Wells, with whom Arnold Bennett first corresponded in 1897, was later very critical of Bennett's work. In his autobiography, Wells adopted a facetious "pottery" metaphor—"[Bennett's] world was as bright and hard surfaced as crockery—his *persona* was, as it were, a hard, definite china figurine"—which allowed Wells to make severe yet superficial judgments of Bennett's writing. Bennett, said Wells, took "the thing that is, for what it was, with a naïve and eager zest. He saw it brighter than it was; he did not see into it and he did not see beyond it." But Bennett, I am arguing, is less a china figurine (or "vessel," in an even less pleasant metaphor)[126] than the bearer of historically determinate aesthetic ideologies, like Wells himself, or any writer. And if Bennett's own practice is that of an "objective" reader of the ideological practices of nineties publishing, one who has cultivated a certain understanding of the publishing sector and has trained him-self to manipulate its distinctive structures in certain ways, so too the novelistic practice of Marie Corelli was that of a writer who manipulated personalized patriarchal practices derived from the new journalism. Hall Caine also produced his novels within the ideological constraints of publishing in the nineties, with yet another version of the realist/ romanticist ideology and a different promotional twist. Indeed, ideo-logically, "publishing" in the nineties was no more than the interplay of the material practices surrounding Hall Caine, Marie Corelli, Arnold Bennett, and countless others. By reading nineties publishing as a deter-minate sector of the social formation, with its determinate aesthetic ideologies and its own particular interplay of the enterprising and list business practices, we can see also that this structure is different from that we discerned in the eighties in the relations of Walter Besant, Henry James, and Robert Louis Stevenson. It is in that difference that we can make out dialectically the transformation of the literary mode of production, tracing itself in ways we have discussed in the often dense concreteness of novel production and ideological production. For the history of novel production at the turn of the century is the history finally of that immense structure, as a process of ordering, broadening, and deepening capital accumulation. We can best know late Victorian publishing as situated in that general historical process, overdetermined by the development of capital elsewhere, as well as determining in its practices the commodities it produces, down to the last details of text, as the texts it produces in turn determine ideologically the possibilities of novel production. In this book I have looked at a few instances of this process; others need to be examined as well, and later ones, as literary capital follows in its own ways its law of accumulation.

Notes
Index

Notes

Preface

1. Louis Althusser, "On Theoretical Work: Difficulties and Resources," *Philosophy and the Spontaneous Philosophy of the Scientists* (London: Verso, 1990), 47.

Chapter 1. Publishing as Capital

1. Karl Marx, "Theses on Feuerbach," *Karl Marx: A Reader*, ed. Jon Elster (Cambridge: Cambridge University Press, 1986), 20.

2. A wider dialectical analysis than I attempt here would trace all mediations of the structures of the social formation, such as the overdeterminations on the economic level of development in printing, typesetting, papermaking, and so on, taking into account, for example, that "the two changes which really mark the watershed between the old and the new are the inventions of photographic block-making and mechanical composition" (Rauri McLean, *Victorian Book Design* [London: Faber, 1963], 160–61); or that "in the quarter century before the Great War the printing industry was in a turmoil of technical and industrial development. The outcome . . . was nothing less than a profound and general change in both the processes of production [technology], and the methods of organization [bilateral collective bargaining, etc.]" (John Child, *Industrial Relations in the British Printing Industry* [London: George Allen & Unwin, 1967], 155).

3. Pierre Bourdieu, *Outline of a Theory of Practice*, trans. R. Nice (Cambridge: Cambridge University Press, 1977), 3.

4. N. N. Feltes, *Modes of Production of Victorian Novels* (Chicago: University of Chicago Press, 1986), 76–77 and passim.

5. Peter Keating, *The Haunted Study: A Social History of the Novel, 1875–1914* (London: Secker and Warburg, 1989), viii–x.

6. Bourdieu, *Outline of a Theory of Practice*, 3.

7. Ernest Mandel, Introduction, Karl Marx, *Capital*, trans. D. Fernbach (Harmondsworth: Penguin, 1981), 3:20.

8. Marx, *Capital* 3:377.

9. *DNB: Supplement, Jan 1901–Dec 1911*, ed. Sidney Lee (London: Smith Elder, 1912), 2:11.

10. Ibid. 2:10.

11. *Times*, 4 October 1890, 10. The original, even stronger, text of Farrar's address is given in *The Official Report of the Church Congress, Held at Hull, on Sept. 30th, and Oct. 1st, 2nd, and 3rd, 1890*, ed. Rev. C. Dunkley (London: Bemrose, 1890), 545–49.

12. *Publishers' Circular*, 53 (15 October 1890), 1352.

13. The *Wellesley Index* lists only Endean's date of birth, but he appears to have been a partner in a firm of London publishers, Kirby and Endean, which published among other things his own *What Is the Eternal Hope of Canon Farrar?* (1878), a critique of Farrar's *Eternal Hope* (1878) consisting of Endean's letters to Farrar interspersed with the notice "Canon Farrar forbids the publication of his letter." Endean and Farrar thus had an ancient grievance.

14. Newman Flower, *Just As It Happened* (London: Cassell, 1950), 78.

15. Simon Nowell-Smith, *The House of Cassell, 1848–1958* (London: Cassell, 1958), 99.

16. *St. James Gazette*, 11 October 1890, 5.

17. *Author*, 1 (15 November 1890), 168.

18. *Bookseller*, 10 October 1890, 1017.

19. *Author*, 1 (15 November 1890), 168.

20. Thomas Dixon Galpin, a retired partner in Cassell's from the time of *The Life of Christ*, challenged Farrar to allow him to make their letters public. *Times*, 13 October 1890, 8.

21. *Publishers' Circular*, 64 (25 April 1896), 444.

22. *Dial*, 24 (16 March 1898), 173.

23. See *The Grievances between Authors and Publishers* (London: Field and Tuer, 1887), 18.

24. *Punch*, 100 (3 January 1891), 2.

25. S. Squire Sprigge, "A Prefatory Note," *The Autobiography of Sir Walter Besant* (London: Hutchinson, 1902), xxiv.

26. S. Smiles, *A Publisher and His Friends: Memoir and Correspondence of the Late John Murray* (London: John Murray, 1891), 2:512. Royal Gettman describes the historical transition from bookseller to publisher in *A Victorian Publisher* (Cambridge: Cambridge University Press, 1960), 1–7.

27. B. Blackwell, *The World of Books: A Panorama* (London: J. M. Dent, 1932), 32.

28. R. Buchanan, *Is Barabbas a Necessity?* (London: Robert Buchanan, 1896), 5.

29. By "reading as structural causality" I mean reading in the way that Marx reads "science" and "the system of machinery" as constituting "the power of the master." *Capital*, trans. B. Fowkes (Harmondsworth: Penguin, 1981), 1:549.

30.   G. H. P. and J. B. P., *Authors and Publishers: A Manual of Suggestions for Beginners in Literature*, 7th ed. (New York and London: G. H. Putnam's Sons, 1897), iv.

31.   *Fifty Years: 1898–1948* (London: Gerald Duckworth, 1948), 7.

32.   William Tinsley, *Random Recollections of an Old Publisher* (London: Simpkin, Marshall, Hamilton, Kent, 1900), 1:309.

33.   *Publishers' Circular*, 64 (25 April 1896), 444; *Author*, 8 (1 October 1897), 114.

34.   Asa Briggs, Introduction, *Essays in the History of Publishing*, ed. Briggs (London: Longman, 1974), 18.

35.   Smiles, *A Publisher and His Friends* 2:516, 515.

36.   Leopold Wagner, *How to Publish a Book or Article* (London: George Redway, 1898), 60.

37.   *Sir Algernon Methuen, Baronet: A Memoir* (London: Methuen, 1925), 9.

38.   Blackwell, *World of Books*, 23.

39.   L. Urwick and E. F. L. Brech, *The Making of Scientific Management* (London: Management Publications Trust, 1946), 2:90.

40.   T. Werner Laurie, "Author, Agent and Publisher: By One of 'The Trade,'" *Nineteenth Century*, 38 (November 1895), 851.

41.   *Grievances between Authors and Publishers*, 9ff.

42.   Ibid., 17.

43.   *Autobiography of Sir Walter Besant*, 218.

44.   Reprinted in William Heinemann, *The Hardships of Publishing* (London: privately printed, 1893), 54–55.

45.   *Grievances between Authors and Publishers*, 17, 25, 27.

46.   John Goode, "The Decadent Writer as Producer," in *Decadence and the 1890s*, ed. Ian Fletcher (London: Edward Arnold, 1979), 119, 118.

47.   Walter Besant, *The Literary Handmaid of the Church* (London: Henry Glaisher, 1890), 4, 3, 10.

48.   *Bookseller*, 13 January 1898, 6.

49.   Laurie, "Author, Agent and Publisher," 855. The *Pall Mall Gazette* wrote that Laurie's paper was "creating some little stir in the publishing trade. We don't seem to recognize the author of the article." *Pall Mall Gazette*, 2 November 1895, "Literary Notes," 4.

50.   Heinemann, *Hardships of Publishing*, 3–4, 99, 100.

51.   Victor Bonham-Carter, *Authors by Profession* (London: Society of Authors, 1978), 1:195.

52.   *The Relation between Author and Publisher from an Authorial Point of View: With Suggestions as to the "Royalty" System*, By a Copyright Holder (London: Printed for the Author, by Wyman & Sons, 1880), 3.

53.   *Publishers' Circular*, 64 (25 April 1896), 444.

54. Alfred Howard, for example, distinguishes "passive copyright, the right to withhold your ideas," from "active copyright, viz., an exclusive right to publish, multiply or diffuse your original intellectual productions" (*Copyright: A Manual for Authors and Publishers* [London: Griffith, Farran, Okeden and Welsh, 1887], 6). Clarence E. Allen labels "competitive copyright" the right existing in childrens' story books, second- and third-rate novels, "and books generally by authors of little repute," and "non-competitive copyright," that right which implies a "monopoly," since "the special privilege of production rests in the hands of an individual who can, . . . according as his reputation is good or second-rate, attach a special price to the article" (*Publishers' Accounts* [London: Gee, 1897], 95–99). That copyright is about control of *text* rather than *book* is suggested by the fact, pointed out by Ian Parsons, that historically the two notions of copyright and censorship developed side by side. "On Copyright," *Essays in the History of Publishing*, 32.

55. See *Bookseller*, 2 June 1905, 485.

56. Charles Morgan, *The House of Macmillan* (London: Macmillan, 1943), 141.

57. *Bookseller*, 7 February 1896, 112.

58. *Author*, 8 (1 December 1897), 187; 10 (1 November 1899), 120.

59. *Publishers' Circular*, 68 (8 January 1898), 34.

60. R. L. Kingsford, *The Publishers' Association: 1896–1946* (Cambridge: Cambridge University Press, 1970), 14.

61. Morgan, *House of Macmillan*, 132; letters, "The Probable Extinction of the Retail Bookseller," *Bookseller*, 6 November 1895, 1077, and 11 December 1895, 1197.

62. *Author*, 6 (1 July 1895), 31, 33.

63. Wagner, *How to Publish*, 63–66; he lists also "manufacturing," or "reprint" publishers, who do not concern us here.

64. F. A. Mumby and Ian Norrie, *Publishing and Bookselling*, 5th ed. (London: Jonathan Cape, 1974), pt. 2, 258, 272.

65. W. Martin Conway, "The Society of Authors: A Reply," *Nineteenth Century*, 38 (December 1895), 976; Wagner, *How to Publish*, 66.

66. Lewis A. Coser, Charles Kadushin, and Walter W. Powell, *Books: The Culture and Commerce of Publishing* (New York: Basic Books, 1982), 36–45; Pierre Bourdieu, *Distinction: A Social Critique of the Judgement of Taste*, trans. R. Nice (London: Routledge and Kegan Paul, 1984), 230. See also Pierre Bourdieu, "La production de la croyance: contribution à une économie des biens symboliques," *Actes de la Recherche en Sciences Sociales*, 13 (Feb. 1972), esp. 23–24.

67. Wagner, *How to Publish*, 70. See also Gettmann's chapter, "The Publisher's Reader," in *Victorian Publisher*.

68. Arthur Waugh, *A Hundred Years of Publishing* (London: Chapman and Hall, 1930), 139.

69. B. W. Matz, "George Meredith as Publisher's Reader," *Fortnightly Review*, 92 (1909), 284; Linda Marie Fritschner, "Publishers' Readers, Publishers, and Their Authors," *Publishing History*, 7 (1980), 48.

70. Waugh, *Hundred Years of Publishing*, 144.

71. Fritschner, "Publishers' Readers," 93, 94.

72. Stanley Unwin, *The Truth about Publishing* (London: George Allen & Unwin, 1926), 24.

73. See *Author*, 4 (1 June 1893), 4; see also James Hepburn, *The Author's Empty Purse and the Rise of the Literary Agent* (Oxford: Oxford University Press, 1968), 55–56, and Robert Colby, "Tale Bearing in the 1890s: *The Author* and Fiction Syndication," *Victorian Periodicals Review*, 18 (Spring 1985), 2–16.

74. Frank Swinnerton, *Authors and the Book Trade* (London: Gerald Howe, 1932), 49.

75. *Author*, 4 (1 December 1893), 240–41, 231.

76. *Author*, 2 (1 April 1892), 348.

77. *Author*, 4 (1 December 1893), 240–41.

78. William Heinemann, "The Middleman as Viewed by a Publisher," *Athenaeum*, 11 November 1893, 663.

79. Frederic Whyte, *William Heinemann: A Memoir* (London: Jonathan Cape, 1928), 127, 126, 128.

80. Laurie, "Author, Agent and Publisher," 852–53. The quarrels over literary agency are discussed in Hepburn, *Author's Empty Purse*, 76–95, and Swinnerton, *Authors and the Book Trade*, 47–59.

81. Sylvia Walby, *Patriarchy at Work: Patriarchal and Capitalist Relations in Employment* (Cambridge: Polity Press, 1986), 50–51.

82. Gaye Tuchman and Nina Fortin, "Edging Women Out: The Structure of Opportunity and the Victorian Novel," *Signs*, 6 (Winter 1980), 308–25; this analysis was developed and supplemented in *Edging Women Out: Victorian Novelists, Publishers, and Social Change* (New Haven: Yale University Press, 1989). I have indicated my reservations about their methods in *JEGP*, 89 (July 1990), 431–34.

83. Walby, *Patriarchy at Work*, 54.

84. Ibid., 56–57.

85. "X. Y. Z.," "Women in Journalism," *Author*, 3 (1 July 1892), 62–63.

86. Walby, *Patriarchy at Work*, 67; "X. Y. Z.," "Women in Journalism," 63.

87. *Author*, 3 (1 July 1892), 46.

88. Wagner, *How to Publish*, 108.

89. *Author*, 8 (1 October 1897), 120.

90. *Times*, 10 October 1890, 10.

91. *Author*, 9 (1 May 1899), 275.

92. Matz, "George Meredith as Publisher's Reader," 285, 289.

93. *Author*, 9 (1 October 1898), 112–13.

94. Frank Swinnerton, "Authors and Advertising," in *Best Sellers: Are They Born or Made*, ed. G. Stevens and S. Unwin (London: George Allen & Unwin, 1939), 112.

95. A. W. Reed, *The Author-Publisher Relationship* (Wellington, N.Z.: published for the P. E. N. by A. H. and A. W. Reed, 1946), 5.

96. Richard De la Mare, *A Publisher on Book Production* (London: Dent, 1936), 12; Richard De la Mare, *Author to Public: Thoughts on the Principles of Book Production* (London: North-Western Polytechnic Printing Department, 1944), 7.

97. Morgan, *House of Macmillan*, 146.

98. Alec Waugh, "About Grant Richards," in Grant Richards, *Author Hunting: Memories of Years Spent Mainly in Publishing*, new ed. (London: Unicorn Press, 1960), xvi.

99. Marx, *Capital* 3:445.

100. Ibid. 3:442, 445–46, 386, 452, 453.

101. Sir Frederic Pollock, *Author*, 9 (1 August 1898), 59.

102. *Academy*, 16 July 1898, 61; *Athenaeum*, 9 July 1898, 68.

103. *Author*, 9 (1 August 1898), 59; 9 (1 September 1898), 82.

104. See *Author*, 4 (1 June 1893), 3.

105. Letter tipped in between pp. 10 and 11 of the Bodleian Library copy of *Forms of Agreement: Issued by the Publishers' Association with Comments by G. Herbert Thring and Illustrative Examples by Sir Walter Besant* (London: Society of Authors, 1903); Shelfmark = 396925.d.1. I am grateful to the Bodleian Library for permission to quote from this letter.

106. *Author*, 10 (1 November 1899), 121.

107. *Author*, 9 (1 November 1898), 134.

108. *Publishers' Circular*, 70 (10 June 1899), 652.

109. *Publishers' Circular*, 70 (25 March 1899), 321.

110. The text of the draft agreements, with Thring's critique in parallel columns and Besant's "Further Comments" appended, were first published in the *Author*, 9 (1 July 1898), 33–49, and reprinted in *Forms of Agreement*.

111. *Author*, 12 (1 June 1901), 3.

112. *Author*, 9 (1 July 1898), 49.

113. *Author*, 13 (1 July 1902), 255; the phrase is misquoted from a mildly ironical poem by Kipling, "The Rhyme of the Three Captains," which was first published during a controversy in 1890. Kipling wrote, referring to an 1881 Besant/Rice novel, "Chaplain of the Fleet—stoutest of them all." *Athenaeum*, 6 December 1890, 776. Obsequies for Besant appeared in *Author*, 12 (1 June 1901), 19–26, and publication was suspended in August and September.

114. Victor Bonham-Carter, *Authors by Profession* (London: Bodley Head and the Society of Authors, 1984), 2:49.

115. G. Herbert Thring, typescript, "History of the Society," British Library Society of Authors Archive, British Library Add. MSS 56869, Vol. 294, pt. 1, 135n. I am grateful to the Society of Authors and to the British Library for permission to quote from this typescript. *The Marketing of Literary Property* was published after Thring's death by Constable and "is still regarded by fellow professionals with respect." Bonham-Carter, *Authors by Profession* 2:40.

116. Robin Myers, *The British Book Trade: From Caxton to the Present Day* (London: Deutsch, 1973), 17.

Chapter 2. Valorizing "the Literary"

1. "The overdetermination of a contradiction is the reflection in it of its conditions of existence within the complex whole, that is, of the other contradictions in the complex whole." Ben Brewster, "Glossary," in Louis Althusser and Étienne Balibar, *Reading Capital*, trans. B. Brewster (London: New Left Books, 1970), 315–16.

2. J. H. Slater, *The Library Manual*, 3d ed. (London: L. Upcott, Gill, 1892), 1, 2–3.

3. Marx's "General Formula for Capital" in *Capital* 1, chap. 4.

4. John Carter and Graham Pollard, *An Enquiry into the Nature of Certain Nineteenth Century Pamphlets* (London: Constable, 1934), 99–100.

5. "The traditional interpretation of the science of bibliography involved the meticulous study of a book *per se* (or of a group of books which have in common certain features of typography, illustration or binding), with only occasional reference to authorship and virtually none to the organization lying behind manufacture and distribution." Michael Sadleir, "The Development During the Last Fifty Years of Bibliographical Study of Books of the XIXth Century," *The Bibliographical Society, 1892–1942: Studies in Retrospect* (London: Bibliographical Society, 1945), 146.

6. James G. Nelson, *The Early Nineties: A View from the Bodley Head* (Cambridge: Harvard University Press, 1971), 78.

7. Historians frequently acknowledge the threat of this sort of corruption: "because a collecting fashion always produces a vociferous horde of speculative hangers-on, the books which a reputable minority really yearned to possess . . . were in danger of appearing to sceptical onlookers mere material for competitive gambling." Sadleir, "Development," 147.

8. John Carter, *Taste and Technique in Book Collecting* (Cambridge: Cambridge University Press, 1948), 1.

9. Sadleir, "Development," 150.

10. Sadleir gives a "Schedule of Bibliographies (in many cases only 'so-called'), Check Lists, Hints to Collectors and so forth attaching to individual English authors of the last century and published during the forty-five years

prior to 1914." The schedule does not claim to be exhaustive but it lists sixty-four items. Ibid., 147, 148.

11. See also Carter and Pollard, *Enquiry*, 108.

12. Sadleir, "Development," 147, 152.

13. J. H. Slater, *Early Editions* (London: Kegan Paul, Trench, Trübner, 1894), vi.

14. *A Catalogue of the Printed Books, Manuscripts, Autograph Letters, Drawings and Pictures, Collected by Frederick Locker-Lampson* (London: Bernard Quaritch, 1886), 153.

15. Carter distinguishes between the "genuine" and the "bogus" in *Taste and Technique*, 101–6. William Roberts sardonically lists such "desirable points" as the canceled and substituted plate of "Rose Maylie and Oliver" in *Oliver Twist*, the suppressed woodcut of the Marquis of Steyne in *Vanity Fair*, and the transposed £ sign in the engraved title of *Martin Chuzzlewit* ("The First Edition Mania," *Fortnightly Review*, 61 [March 1894], 348).

16. J. H. Slater, *The Romance of Book-Collecting* (London: Elliot Stock, 1898), 113, 115.

17. J. H. Slater, *Book-Collecting: A Guide for Amateurs* (London: Swan Sonnenschein, 1892), 9.

18. William Swan Sonnenschein, *The Best Books: A Reader's Guide to the Choice of the Best Available Books (About 25,000) in Every Department of Science, Art and Literature . . . ; A Contribution Towards Classified Bibliography* (London: Swan Sonnenschein Lowery, 1887), iii–iv, iii.

19. *DNB* (1912–1921), 345–47.

20. "Sir John Lubbock on Reading," *Morning Advertiser*, 11 January 1886, 2; Sir John Lubbock, "On the Pleasure of Reading," *Contemporary Review*, 49 (February 1886), 240–51; *The Pleasures of Life*, 3d ed. (London: Macmillan, 1887).

21. *Archives of Macmillan and Co.* (Cambridge: Chadwyck-Healey, 1982), Out Letterbooks 543 (R. & R. Clark Printers, 1887–1889, 31 May to 12 December 1889), Reel 23. I am grateful to Macmillan Publishers, Ltd., for permission to quote from the Macmillan Archive in the British Library and to Chadwyck-Healey, Ltd., for permission to quote from their microfilm edition of those papers. The long successful publishing history of *The Pleasures of Life* is indicated in *A Bibliographical Catalogue of Macmillan and Co.'s Publications from 1843 to 1889* (London: Macmillan, 1891), 518.

22. Although initially they were prepared to dismiss it as "a railway ride through human culture, with ten minutes stoppage at all the principal stations." "Sir John Lubbock's Liberal Education," *Pall Mall Gazette*, 42 (11 January 1886), 4. Hereafter cited as *PMG*.

23. *The Henry James Letters*, ed. L. Edel (Cambridge: Harvard University Press, 1980), 3:108–9; *The Best Hundred Books by the Best Judges*, *PMG*

"Extra," no. 24 (London: "Pall Mall Gazette" Office, 1886), 8. Hereafter cited as "Extra."

24. "What to Read," *Saturday Review*, 61 (23 January 1886), 106.

25. *Publishers' Circular*, 49 (1 April 1886), 339.

26. *Publishers' Circular*, 49 (15 June 1886), 655.

27. Lubbock, "On the Pleasure of Reading" 246n; James Pycroft, *A Course of English Reading Adapted to Every Taste and Capacity with Anecdotes of Men of Genius* (London: Longman, 1844; 4th ed., 1861); James Baldwin, *The Book Lover: A Guide to the Best Reading* (London: Putnam, 1844; 14th ed., 1902).

28. "An Old Book Lover," *The Best Books: A List for the Guidance of General Readers* (Sheffield: Leader and Sons, 1886), 3.

29. Frederic Harrison, "On the Choice of Books," *Fortnightly*, n.s. 25 (April 1879), 491–512, revised for *The Choice of Books and Other Literary Pieces* (London: Macmillan, 1886).

30. "A Desultory Reader" [S. G. G.], "The Best Hundred Books: First Paper," *Leisure Hour*, 35 (1886), 268.

31. *Athenaeum*, 20 March 1886, 383.

32. "An Old Book Lover," *Best Books*, 4.

33. R. H. Super, "Critical and Explanatory Notes," *English Literature and Irish Politics, The Complete Prose Works of Matthew Arnold*, ed. Super (Ann Arbor: University of Michigan Press, 1973), 9:347, 380–81.

34. Matthew Arnold, "The Study of Poetry," *English Literature and Irish Politics, Complete Prose Works* 9:170, 161; "On Poetry," ibid., 63.

35. Matthew Arnold, "Culture and Anarchy," *Culture and Anarchy with Friendship's Garland and Some Literary Essays, Complete Prose Works* 5:113; originally "criticism" in "The Function of Criticism at the Present Time," *Lectures and Essays in Criticism, Complete Prose Works* 3:283.

36. Simon Nowell-Smith, *The House of Cassell* (London: Cassell, 1958), 109.

37. *Publishers' Circular*, 49 (1 March 1886), 198.

38. *Times*, 20 March 1886, 15; 22 March 1886, 12; 23 March 1886, 10; reprinted in *Publishers' Circular*, 49 (1 April 1886), 317–18. See also Nowell-Smith, *House of Cassell*, 108–11.

39. Lubbock's covering letter says, "I will write to Macmillan." *The Archives of George Routledge & Co, 1853–1902*, ed. B. Maidment (London: Chadwyck-Healey, 1973), Reel 3: Contracts c.1887–98/99, 2 (L–Z):40. I am grateful to Routledge and to International Thompson Publishing Services, Ltd., for permission to quote from the Routledge Archive and to Chadwyck-Healey, Ltd., for permission to quote from their microfilm edition.

40. John Lubbock, Introduction, *Herodotus*, trans. H. Cary (London: G. Routledge, 1891), 4. In 1904 it was pointed out that the duodecimal equivalent of "100" was more accurately "144."

41. *Bohn's Libraries Catalogue* (n.d., 1890s), 1–5; "Booksellers' and Publishers' Shortlists," John Johnson Collection, Bodleian Library, Oxford, file 16.

42. John Locke, *An Essay concerning the Human Understanding* (London: G. Routledge, 1894); *Routledge Archives*, Publications Books, 1853–1902, Vol. 16; *The Hundred Best Books in the World of Literature as Selected by Sir John Lubbock, Bart.* (London: Harmsworth Brothers, 1899); "The Best Hundred Books/Revised Version/Lord Avebury's New List," PMG, 4 June 1904, 7, corrected as "Lord Avebury's Final List," PMG, 6 June 1904, 3.

43. PMG, 15 June 1904, 4. Max Beerbohm's letter echoed Wilde's of eighteen years earlier: "A year or two ago in the Strand a large poster caught my gaze. It bore the imprimatur of the Young Men's Christian Association and it depicted a young Christian man, in a suit of deep mourning, reading from a small black book, which he held in both hands. On the back of the book was printed in white letters the title. The title was, quite simply, "Greek." As a lover of the human comedy in all its manifestations, I have always wished to possess a copy of this poster. Lord Avebury's revised list of the Hundred Best Books will do instead." PMG, 11 June 1904, 7.

44. "Claudius Clear," *A Library for Five Pounds* (London: Hodder & Stoughton, 1917), 11.

45. *The Life-Work of Lord Avebury (Sir John Lubbock), 1834–1913*, ed. Mrs. A. Grant Duff (London: Watts, 1924), 232.

46. PMG, 4 June 1904, 7.

47. Annette Kuhn and Ann-Marie Wolpe, editorial preface to Roisin McDonough and Rachel Harrison, "Patriarchy and Relations of Production," in *Feminism and Materialism*, ed. A. Kuhn and A.-M. Wolpe (London: Routledge and Kegan Paul, 1978), 12.

48. Zillah Eisenstein, "Developing a Theory of Capitalist Patriarchy and Socialist Feminism," in *Capitalist Patriarchy and the Case for Socialist Feminism*, ed. Z. R. Eisenstein (New York: Monthly Review Press, 1979), 28.

49. Sylvia Walby, *Patriarchy at Work* (Cambridge: Polity Press, 1986), 56.

50. Elaine Showalter, *A Literature of Their Own*, new rev. ed. (London: Virago, 1982), 75–82.

51. G. H. Lewes, "The Lady Novelists," *Westminster Review*, n.s. 2 (1852), 133.

52. Walby, *Patriarchy at Work*, 55–56.

53. Zillah Eisenstein, Introduction, *Capitalist Patriarchy*, 5.

54. Dale Spender, *Mothers of the Novel* (London: Pandora Press, 1986), 162.

55. See Inga-Stina Ewbank, *Their Proper Sphere: A Study of the Brontë Sisters as Early-Victorian Female Novelists* (London: Edward Arnold, 1966), 13ff.

56. Margaret Shaw, "Constructing the 'Literate Woman': Nineteenth-Century Reviews and Emerging Literacies," *Dickens Studies Annual* (Fall 1992).

57. Jean Ferguson Carr, "Writing as a Woman: Dickens, *Hard Times*, and Feminine Discourses," *Dickens Studies Annual*, 18 (1989), 161, 162.

58. Kenneth Graham, *English Criticism of the Novel, 1865–1900* (Oxford: Clarendon Press, 1965), 63ff.

59. R. L. Stevenson, "A Humble Remonstrance," *Longman's Magazine*, 5 (1884–85), 142–43, collected in *The Works of Robert Louis Stevenson*, Vailima Ed. (New York: Scribner's, 1922), 12:213.

60. Spender, *Mothers of the Novel*, 157.

61. Eleanor Marx Aveling and Edward Aveling, "The Woman Question— From a Socialist Point of View," *Westminster Review*, n.s. 69 (January 1886), 211.

62. See Showalter, *Literature of Their Own*, 73ff.; Gaye Tuchman and Nina Fortin, *Edging Women Out: Victorian Novelists, Publishers, and Social Change* (New Haven: Yale University Press, 1989), 175ff.

63. Tuchman and Fortin, *Edging Women Out*, 47, 7–8.

64. Shaw, "Constructing the 'Literate Woman.'"

65. Fredric Jameson, *The Political Unconscious* (Ithaca: Cornell University Press, 1981), 214.

66. Brander Matthews, "Cheap Books and Good Books," in *The Question of Copyright*, ed. G. H. Putnam (London: G. P. Putnam's Sons, 1891), 346.

67. Ibid., 345–46.

68. Sam Ricketson, *The Berne Convention for the Protection of Literary and Artistic Works, 1886–1986* (London: Centre for Commercial Law Studies, Queen Mary College/Kluwer, 1987), 5, 22, 30, 39.

69. Ibid., 41–71; R. R. Bowker, *Copyright: Its History and Its Law* (London: Constable, 1912), 311–21; W. Briggs, *The Law of International Copyright* (London: Stevens and Haynes, 1906), 232–41.

70. W. A. Copinger, *The Law of Copyright in Works of Literature and Art*, 3d ed. (London: Stevens and Haynes, 1893), 567, 578–580; Briggs, *Law of International Copyright*, 640–50.

71. Bowker, *Copyright*, 251.

72. Brander Matthews, "The Evolution of Copyright," in *Question of Copyright*, 29 n. 1.

73. Ricketson, *Berne Convention*, 18.

74. *Parliamentary Papers. Reports: Commissioners, Inspectors and Others.* Report of the Commissioners appointed to make Inquiry with regard to the laws and regulations relating to home, Colonial and International Copyrights: Minutes of Evidence, Session 17 January–16 August 1878, 24:260. Hereafter cited as *RC; OED*.

75. S. S. Conant, "International Copyright: I. An American View," *Macmillan's Magazine*, 40 (1879), 153; Simon Nowell-Smith, *International Copyright Law and the Publisher in the Reign of Queen Victoria* (Oxford: Clarendon Press,

1968), 77; see also Arnold Plant, "The Economic Aspects of Copyright on Books," *Economica*, 1 (1934), 167–95.

76. David Harvey, *The Condition of Postmodernity* (Oxford: Basil Blackwell, 1989), 216.

77. Augustine Birrell, *Seven Lectures on the Law and History of Copyright in Books* (London: Cassell, 1899), 213.

78. [J. A. Froude], review of *Report of the Copyright Commission . . . 1878; Minutes of the Evidence taken before the Royal Commission on Copyright . . . 1878*, *Edinburgh Review*, 148 (October 1878), 329.

79. Conant, "International Copyright," 153.

80. [L. H. Courteney], "International Copyright: II. An Englishman's View of the Foregoing," *Macmillan's Magazine*, 40 (1879), 163. For a survey of the geographical and demographic determinations of late-nineteenth-century American publishing see William Charvat's "The People's Patronage," in *The Profession of Authorship in America, 1800–1870: The Papers of William Charvat*, ed. Matthew J. Bruccoli (Columbus: Ohio State University Press, 1968).

81. Froude, review of *Report*, 314.

82. Nowell-Smith, *International Copyright Law*, 65–66.

83. Ibid., 34–35.

84. *Articles of the International Copyright Union* (London: Longman's, Green, 1887), 20.

85. Froude, review of *Report*, 342.

86. Harvey, *Condition of Postmodernity*, 226, 232. This whole section, especially this paragraph, is heavily influenced by Harvey's discussion of "The Experience of Space and Time," part 3 of *The Condition of Postmodernity*. Harvey's methods open the possibility of a detailed analysis of spatial and temporal practices of modern capitalist publishing. His "grid of spatial practices," for instance, drawing on Henri Lefebvre's *La production de l'espace* (1974), allows one to analyze spatially the ideological position of late Victorian publishing: the Berne Convention as a "representation of space," a signification that allows "such material practices to be talked about and understood," or Free Trade as a "space of representation," a "mental invention," allowing one to "imagine new meanings or possibilities for spatial practices." His use of "Gurvich's typology of social times" similarly enriches the concepts of "list" and "entrepreneurial" publishing (218–25).

87. Froude, review of *Report*, 309.

88. Bernard Mallett, Introduction, in Sir Louis Mallett, *Free Exchange* (London: Kegan Paul, Trench, Trübner, 1891), vi.

89. *DNB* 12:872.

90. *DNB*, Supplement 22:627.

91. *RC*, 581.

92. T. H. Farrar, *Free Trade Versus Fair Trade* (London: Cassell, Petter, Galpin, 1882), 86.

93. RC, 303, 304.

94. Ibid., 540.

95. Ibid., 406, 460, 468.

96. Ibid., 520–21.

97. Ibid., 520.

98. Froude, review of *Report*, 339.

99. RC, 520.

100. T. H. Farrar, "The Principle of Copyright," *Fortnightly Review*, 30 (1878), 842, 843.

101. Ibid., 848, 846.

Chapter 3. The Process of Literary Capital in the 1880s

1. Mark Spilka, "Henry James and Walter Besant: 'The Art of Fiction' Controversy," *Novel*, 6 (Winter 1973), 101. John Goode points out that Hardy drafted an essay with the same title in 1881. John Goode, "The Art of Fiction: Walter Besant and Henry James," *Tradition and Tolerance in Nineteenth Century Fiction*, ed. D. Howard, J. Lucas, and J. Goode (London: Routledge and Kegan Paul, 1966), 245.

2. Spilka, "James and Besant," 102.

3. *Encyclopedia Britannica*, 11th ed. (Cambridge: Cambridge University Press), 25:309. The 1799 proposal was for "a public institution for diffusing the knowledge and facili[t]ating the general introduction of useful mechanical inventions and improvements, and for teaching by courses of philosophical lectures and experiments the application of science to the common purposes of life." Bence Jones, *The Royal Institution* (1871; rpt. New York: Arno Press 1975), 121.

4. Gwendy Caroe, *The Royal Institution: An Informal History* (London: John Murray, 1985), 69.

5. Ibid., 92.

6. Walter Besant, *The Art of Fiction* (London: Chatto and Windus, 1884), 3–4, 16, 21, 24, 25.

7. Spilka, "James and Besant," 109.

8. Bruce R. McElderry, Jr., "Henry James's 'The Art of Fiction,'" *Research Studies of the State College of Washington*, 25 (March 1957), 94.

9. Walter Besant, *Autobiography* (London: Hutchinson, 1902), 216.

10. Goode, "Art of Fiction," 246.

11. Spilka, "James and Besant," 107.

12. Goode, "Art of Fiction," 249.

13. Spilka, "James and Besant," 104.

14. Goode, "Art of Fiction," 253.

15. Walter Besant, "On the Writing of Novels," *Atalanta*, 1 (December 1887), 163.

16. Walter Besant, Preface to a New Edition, *All Sorts and Conditions of Men*, new ed. (Toronto: Macmillan, 1910), vii.

17. Simon Eliot, "'His Generation Read His Stories': Walter Besant, Chatto and Windus and *All Sorts and Conditions of Men*," *Publishing History*, 21 (1987), 37–41.

18. *Times*, 26 December 1882, 5.

19. *Fortnightly Review*, 40 (1883), 880, 881.

20. *Nation*, 36 (1883), 41.

21. In my ideological analyses of novels I am adapting freely Fredric Jameson's own adaptation of A. J. Greimas' "semiotic square" in *The Political Unconscious* (Ithaca: Cornell University Press, 1981), 46–48, 83.

22. Goode, "Art of Fiction," 255.

23. Walter Besant, *All Sorts and Conditions of Men: An Impossible Story* (London: Chatto and Windus, 1884), 136. Further references are to this edition.

24. Fred W. Boege, "Sir Walter Besant, Novelist: Part One," *Nineteenth Century Fiction*, 10 (1956), 258.

25. See Michael McKeon, *The Origins of the English Novel* (Baltimore: Johns Hopkins University Press, 1987), 56–57.

26. "Appendix: Table I.—Classification and Description of the Population of London, 1887–1889, by School Board Blocks and Divisions," Map 76a: Mile End Old Town, in Charles Booth, *Life and Labour of the People in London*, First Series: Poverty (New York: AMS Press, [1970]), 1:30. Booth there describes the neighborhood: "Densely crowded block round the London Hospital. Two-thirds of the inhabitants are in steady work, and their weekly wages, if small, are regular. A certain amount of prostitution and its accompanying evils in some of the streets." Yet Jane Stuart-Wortley regretted "that a writer of Mr Besant's brilliant powers should present pictures of this portion of London which, by systematic suppression of all its more hopeful features, are distinctly unfair." "The East End as Represented by Mr Besant," *Nineteenth Century*, 22 (September 1887), 362. P. J. Keating discusses "the changing attitude of novelists towards the East End" in *The Working Classes in Victorian Fiction* (London: Routledge & Kegan Paul, 1971), 121–24.

27. Besant's attitude toward radicalism is indicated in his satiric poem "The Day is Coming. By W——m M——s":

> For strong and for weak alike, for good as well as for bad,
> An equal reward shall be meted, and an equal wage be paid.
> Then the cry of the rough will be "Grab!" and the cry
>   of the poor, "Divide!"
> And no man shall have any money, and no man shall
>   have any pride.

Recreations of the Rabelais Club, 1881–1885 (Guilford: Billing and Son, Printers, 1885), 22.

28. Besant, *Autobiography*, 284.

29. Boege, "Sir Walter Besant," 272.

30. "*Temple Bar*: Introduction," in *The Wellesley Index of Victorian Periodicals*, ed. W. E. Houghton and E. R. Houghton (Toronto: University of Toronto Press, 1979), 3:386, 387.

31. Eliot, "His Generation," 28–29.

32. Ibid., 29, 28, 34, 35.

33. Ibid., 30, 34, 35.

34. Boege, "Sir Walter Besant," 259.

35. Edith Sichel, "Two Philanthropic Novelists: Mr Walter Besant and Mr George Gissing," *Murray's Magazine*, 3 (1888), 515.

36. Goode, "Art of Fiction," 244.

37. Eliot, "His Generation," 35, 36.

38. Leon Edel, ed., *The Henry James Letters* (Cambridge: Harvard University Press, 1980), 3:194.

39. F. L. Mott, "The Atlantic Monthly," *A History of American Magazines, 1850–1865* (Cambridge: Harvard University Press, 1938), 2:511.

40. Lang's review was reprinted in *The Critic and Good Literature*, 1, n.s. (24 May 1884), 249–50. See also Oscar Maurer, "Andrew Lang and Longman's Magazine, 1882–1905," *University of Texas Studies in English*, 34 (1955), 152–78.

41. "Longman's Magazine," *Wellesley Index* 4:430, 433, 431, 435.

42. Henry James, "The Art of Fiction" [1884 text], in Janet Adam Smith, *Henry James and Robert Louis Stevenson: A Record of Their Friendship and Criticism* (London: Rupert Hart-Davis, 1948), 78. Page references in my text refer to this edition.

43. Edel, *James Letters* 3:240.

44. Spilka, "James and Besant," 109.

45. Taylor Stoehr, "Words and Deeds in *The Princess Casamassima*," *ELH*, 37 (1970), 111.

46. Henry James, Preface, *The Princess Casamassima*, ed. Derek Brewer (London: Penguin, 1977), 33. All page references are to this edition of the 1886 text.

47. Michael Anesko, *"Friction with the Market": Henry James and the Profession of Authorship* (New York: Oxford University Press, 1986), 229 n. 25.

48. See also James, "Art of Fiction," 75.

49. John Lucas considers Lady Aurora "one of the finest things in *The Princess Casamassima*, for James sees with absolute sureness the pathetic and comic futility of her desire for service." "Conservatism and Revolution in the 1880s," in *Literature and Politics in the Nineteenth Century*, ed. Lucas (London: Methuen, 1971), 211.

50. Goode, "Art of Fiction," 274.

51. This is apparently the date of the novel's action (see 603 n. 175).

52. Goode, "Art of Fiction," 275. Martha Nussbaum argues to the contrary in "Perception and Revolution: *The Princess Casamassima* and the Political Imagination," in *Meaning and Method: Essays in Honor of Hilary Putnam*, ed. G. Boolos (Cambridge: Cambridge University Press, 1990), 327–53.

53. Leon Edel and Dan H. Lawrence, *A Bibliography of Henry James*, 3d ed. (Oxford: Clarendon Press, 1982), 75–76.

54. See Anesko, "*Friction with the Market*," 36.

55. Eliot, "His Generation," 38.

56. Charles Morgan, *The House of Macmillan* (London: Macmillan, 1943), 102.

57. *A Bibliographical Catalogue of Macmillan and Co.'s Publications from 1843 to 1889* (London: Macmillan, 1891), 497.

58. Edel, *James Letters* 3:102.

59. Edel and Lawrence, *Bibliography*, 76; Eliot, "His Generation," 37–40.

60. Morgan, *House of Macmillan*, 101.

61. Edel and Lawrence, *Bibliography*, 76.

62. I have not collated every subsequent edition of *The Princess Casamassima*, but the New York and the Penguin Classics editions follow the book divisions of the three-decker. In both formats books 1 and 2 are the same, but in the serial book 3 ends with chapter 32, and book 6 becomes book 5.

63. *The Complete Notebooks of Henry James*, ed. L. Edel and L. H. Powers (New York: Oxford University Press, 1987), 31.

64. Deborah Esch, "Promissory Notes: The Prescription of the Future in *The Princess Casamassima*," *American Literary History*, 1 (Summer 1989), 325.

65. Smith, *James and Stevenson*, 101, 102.

66. R. L. Stevenson, "A Humble Remonstrance," *The Works of Robert Louis Stevenson*, Vailima Ed. (New York: Scribner's, 1922), 12:206–7. All references to Stevenson's essays are to this edition.

67. Stevenson's essay was one of a series written for the first "*British Weekly* Extra" in 1877 and collected in *Books Which Have Influenced Me* (London: Hodder & Stoughton, 1897). The Prefatory Note to the 1897 volume states that the first paper of the series appeared on 28 June 1887: "It had been arranged for some time previously. This will be found to settle any question of priority" (v). The reference seems to be to the *Pall Mall Gazette*'s "Hundred Best Books."

68. In October 1883, he wrote to his cousin: "I have written a breathless note on Realism for Henley; a fifth part of the subject hurriedly touched, which will show you how my thoughts are driving." "The Letters of Robert Louis Stevenson," *Works* 21:220.

69. As in "On Some Technical Elements of Style in Literature," Ibid., 4:424–50, first published in *Contemporary Review*, 47 (April 1885), 548–61.

70. Roger G. Swearingen, *The Prose Writings of Robert Louis Stevenson: A Guide* (Hamden, Conn.: Archon Books, 1980), 98; W. F. Prideaux, *A Bibliography of the Works of Robert Louis Stevenson*, 2d ed. (1917; New York: Burt Franklin, 1968), 44.

71. *Archives of the House of Longman, 1794–1914* (Cambridge: Chadwyck-Healey, 1978), Reel 30: Royalty Ledger, 1884–1905, entry 317. I am grateful to Longman Group UK Limited for permission to cite the Longman Archive and to Chadwyck-Healey, Ltd., for permission to cite their edition of the Longman Archive. Swearingen, *Prose Writings*, 99.

72. Graham Balfour, *The Life of Robert Louis Stevenson*, 4th ed. (London: Methuen, 1908), 230.

73. Swearingen, *Prose Writings*, 98; Balfour, *Life*, 230; George L. McKay, *Some Notes on Robert Louis Stevenson: His Finances, and His Agents and Publishers* (New Haven: Yale University Library, 1958), 19.

74. *Athenaeum*, 30 January 1886, 157; 27 February 1886, 285; 3 April 1886, 497.

75. Harold Orel, *The Victorian Short Story* (Cambridge: Cambridge University Press, 1986), 123.

76. Balfour, *Life*, 230.

77. *Longman Archives*, Reel 30: Royalty Ledger 1884–1905, entry 184r.

78. McKay, *Some Notes*, 24, 22.

79. *Times*, 2 April 1887, 6.

80. McKay, *Some Notes*, 19; *Longman Archives*, Reel 30: Royalty Ledger 1884–1905, entry 184r, "Memorandum from Longmans, Green, New York, to Mr. Masters, 20 September 1889."

81. Paul Maixner, Introduction, *Robert Louis Stevenson: The Critical Heritage* (London: Routledge and Kegan Paul, 1981), 22–23.

82. Balfour, *Life*, 243.

83. Barry Menikoff, *Robert Louis Stevenson and "The Beach at Falesá"* (Stanford: Stanford University Press, 1984), 32.

84. J. H. Slater, *Early Editions* (London: Kegan Paul, Trench, Trübner, 1894), 275; J. H. Slater, *Robert Louis Stevenson: A Bibliography of His Complete Works* (London: G. Bell, 1914), 37. An American collector records that Stevenson first editions were being collected in 1889–90, that is, during Stevenson's lifetime. W. D. Ellwanger, "The Collecting of Stevensons," *Bachelor of Arts: A Monthly Magazine Devoted to University Interests and General Literature* [New York], 1 (July–August 1895), 346–47.

85. John Carter and Graham Pollard, *An Enquiry Into the Nature of Certain Nineteenth Century Pamphlets* (London: Constable, 1934), 247, 254, 251.

W. F. Prideaux appears to have accepted the word of his friend T. J. Wise for the authenticity of these works for his *Bibliography*.

86. Menikoff, *Stevenson and "Falesá,"* 8–9.

87. Ibid., 8.

88. Henry James, "Robert Louis Stevenson," in Smith, *James and Stevenson*, 156. This essay was published in the *Century* (April 1888).

89. Elaine Showalter, *Sexual Anarchy: Gender and Culture at the Fin de Siècle* (New York: Viking Penguin, 1990), 107.

90. Robert Louis Stevenson, *The Strange Case of Dr. Jekyll and Mr. Hyde and Other Stories*, ed. Jenni Calder (London: Penguin, 1979), 43. All page references are to this edition of the 1886 text.

91. Smith, *James and Stevenson*, 151.

92. "So good an artist in fanciful mysteries as Mr. Stevenson should have avoided the mistake of a lengthy rationalization at all," wrote E. T. Cook, in merely the first of several such objections (*Athenaeum*, 16 January 1886, 100). See also Elizabeth MacAndrew, *The Gothic Tradition in Fiction* (New York: Columbia University Press, 1979), 52, and J. R. Hammond, *A Robert Louis Stevenson Companion* (London: Macmillan, 1984), 122.

93. Edward Eigner, *Robert Louis Stevenson and Romantic Tradition* (Princeton: Princeton University Press, 1966), 18.

94. See ibid., 143–44.

95. Louis Althusser, "Ideology and Ideological State Apparatuses," *Lenin and Philosophy*, trans. B. Brewster (London: Verso, 1971), 152.

Chapter 4. The Process of Literary Capital in the 1890s

1. Louis Althusser, "On Theoretical Work: Difficulties and Resources," *Philosophy and the Spontaneous Philosophy of the Scientists*, ed. G. Elliott (London: Verso, 1990), 48.

2. William C. Frierson, "The English Controversy over Realism in Fiction, 1885–1895," *PMLA*, 43 (1928), 549, 545.

3. Wilbur Cross, *The Development of the English Novel* (1899; New York: Macmillan, 1932), 288. "He had a detestable influence on fiction," wrote Rebecca West. "Backed up by Gosse and Andrew Lang, he established romanticism as the current fashion. In the hands of his imitators it became thinner and thinner, and more of a trivial decoration." *Arnold Bennett Himself*, John Day Pamphlet no. 1 (New York: John Day, 1931), 14.

4. John Gross, *The Rise and Fall of the Man of Letters* (London: Weidenfield and Nicolson, 1969), 135.

5. In 1890, Hall Caine proposed almost a semiotic square *avant la lettre*, constructed from the manifest contraries "realism/idealism." Along with these manifest contraries he suggested a pair of latent contraries: "the real pitfall

of realism—cynicism" and "the true consort of imagination . . . , enthusiasm." "The New Watchwords of Fiction," *Contemporary Review*, 57 (April 1890), 480–81. What prevents this from anticipating a true semiotic square is the omission of any *contradictory* relations. To recognize the *contradiction* between realism and idealism, as does my square, and especially that between romance and the forms of empiricism, is both to escape Caine's moralism and incidentally to gesture toward the historical "motor" driving the change in the actual social formation.

6. Kenneth Graham, *English Criticism of the Novel: 1865–1900* (Oxford: Clarendon Press, 1965), 66.

7. "Realism and Romance," *Contemporary Review*, 52 (November 1887), 683–93; "A New Novelist," *Westminster Review*, 128 (October 1887), 840–49; "The Difficulty of Romance-Writers," *Spectator*, 61 (21 January 1888), 88–89; Maurice Thompson, "The Domain of Romance," *Forum*, 8 (November 1889), 326–36; James Sully, "The Future of Fiction," *Forum*, 9 (August 1890), 644–47; Mary D. Cutting, "Two Forces in Fiction," *Forum*, 10 (October 1890), 216–25; Hall Caine, "The New Watchwords of Fiction," *Contemporary Review*, 57 (April 1890), 479–88; Edmund Gosse, "The Limits of Realism in Fiction," *Forum*, 9 (June 1890), 391–400; H. Traill, "Romance Realisticized," *Contemporary Review*, 59 (February 1891), 200–209; "English Realism and Romance," *Quarterly Review*, 173 (October 1891), 468–94. In passing I might note the occurrence of titles containing the word "romance" in articles indexed in three volumes of *Poole's Index*: *1882–87*, 17; *1887–92*, 26; *1892–97*, 30. Similarly, the *English Catalogue of Books* records three "romance" titles between 1881 and 1889, and fifty-three (and a "Romance Library") between 1890 and 1897.

8. Andrew Lang, "Tendencies in Fiction," *North American Review*, 161 (August 1895), 154–55.

9. H. Rider Haggard, "About Fiction," *Contemporary Review*, 51 (February 1887), 172–80. Mowbray Morris, commenting in the March *Macmillan's*, focuses on Haggard's remarks on "candor" ("Some Thoughts about Novels," *Macmillan's Magazine*, 55 [March 1887], 358–65).

10. Andrew Lang, "Realism and Romance," *Contemporary Review*, 52 (November 1887), 683–93.

11. George Saintsbury, "The Present State of the Novel: I," *Fortnightly Review*, n.s. 42 (September 1887), 410–17.

12. George Saintsbury, "The Present State of the Novel: II," *Fortnightly Review*, n.s. 43 (January 1888), 122.

13. Stephen Potter, *The Muse in Chains: A Study in Education* (London: Jonathan Cape, 1937), 126, 130.

14. *Wellesley Index* 2:176, 1:212.

15. Graham, *English Criticism*, 69.

16. "Candour in English Fiction," *New Review*, 2 (January 1890), 6–21. Besant's contribution covered pp. 6–9, Linton's pp. 10–14 and Hardy's pp. 15–21. I shall refer to them in the text by page number; Graham, *English Criticism*, 94.

17. *Wellesley Index* 3:303.

18. "A New Novelist," *Westminster Review*, 128 (October 1887), 840, 842, 843.

19. F. A. Mumby and Ian Norrie, *Publishing and Bookselling*, 5th ed. rev. (London: Jonathan Cape, 1974), 276.

20. Frederic Whyte, *William Heinemann: A Memoir* (London: Jonathan Cape, 1928), 77, 89; Mumby and Norrie, *Publishing and Bookselling*, 277.

21. "Tillotson's Agreement Books," Bodleian MS Eng. Misc. f. 395/1, 1:1–6. I am grateful to Dr. Paul O'Flinn for obtaining this information for me.

22. *Athenaeum*, 4 January 1890, 31. In the same issue *Athenaeum* noted that Heinemann was "not altogether unknown to literary men owing to his connexion for the last ten years with the business of Trübner & Co" (19).

23. *Athenaeum*, 18 January 1890, 98; 1 February 1890, 163.

24. Simon Nowell-Smith, *The House of Cassell, 1848–1958* (London: Cassell, 1958), 189; Whyte, *Heinemann*, 54.

25. *Athenaeum*, 7 February 1890, 195.

26. *Athenaeum*, 8 March 1890, 323.

27. *Athenaeum*, 15 March 1890, 355; *Academy* 37 (1 March 1890), 147.

28. *Athenaeum*, 25 October 1890, 560; 3 January 1891, 34.

29. Caine, "New Watchwords of Fiction" 488, 485.

30. John St. John, *William Heinemann: A Century of Publishing 1890–1990* (London: Heinemann, 1990), 9.

31. Edmund Gosse, "Heinemann's International Library," *Athenaeum*, 24 May 1890, 662.

32. Mumby and Norrie, *Publishing and Bookselling*, 278.

33. Whyte, *Heinemann*, 36.

34. *Athenaeum*, 25 October 1890, 560; 28 March 1891, 422; compare *Daily Telegraph*, 25 October 1895, 2, and *Pall Mall Gazette*, 17 October 1895, 9.

35. *Athenaeum*, 28 July 1894, 115.

36. *Athenaeum*, 14 March 1891, 336.

37. Quoted and commented on in the *Saturday Review*, 78 (17 November 1894), 530. Caine would seem to have had the same dream, over a year later, before a student audience at the University of Pennsylvania. See *Critic*, 27 (23 November 1895), 355.

38. Hall Caine, *My Story* (London: Heinemann, 1908), 283.

39. Whyte, *Heinemann*, 53.

40. "Recent Novels," *Times*, 8 March 1890, 15.

41. Hall Caine, *The Bondman: A New Saga* (London: Heinemann, 1890), 1:204. All page references in the text are to this edition.

42. "A New Novelist," 848.

43. "New Novels," *Academy*, 37 (1 March 1890), 147; "Recent Novels," *Times*, 8 March 1890, 15.

44. *Wellesley Index* 3:387.

45. Brian Masters, *Now Barabbas Was a Rotter: The Extraordinary Life of Marie Corelli* (London: Hamish Hamilton, 1978), 49–51. See also George Bullock, *Marie Corelli: The Life and Death of a Best-Seller* (London: Constable, 1940), 36–37, and Eileen Bigland, *Marie Corelli: The Woman and the Legend* (London: Jarrolds, 1953), 65–66.

46. Masters, *Barabbas*, 54–55; Bigland, *Corelli*, 73.

47. Masters, *Barabbas*, 55; see also Bullock, *Corelli*, 41.

48. Bigland, *Corelli*, 77; Bullock, *Corelli*, 42–44.

49. Masters, *Barabbas*, 59.

50. Ibid., 66.

51. *Athenaeum*, 9 October 1886, 456; Bigland, *Corelli*, 87.

52. Masters, *Barabbas*, 113.

53. Royal Gettmann, *A Victorian Publisher: A Study of the Bentley Papers* (Cambridge: Cambridge University Press, 1960), 26.

54. The fullest account of this episode is Masters' chapter "The Break with Bentley," *Barabbas*, 113–26. Publicly, Marie Corelli said simply, "A change of publishers is sometimes advisable." Marie Corelli, "My First Book," *Idler*, 4 (1893), 244.

55. *Athenaeum*, 7 October 1893, 480; Michael Sadleir, *XIX Century Fiction* (Cambridge: Cambridge University Press, 1951), 2:108.

56. *Athenaeum*, 18 November 1893, 680; 2 December 1893, 754.

57. Mumby and Norrie, *Publishing and Bookselling*, 279; Maureen Duffy, *A Thousand Capricious Chances: A History of the Methuen List, 1889–1989* (London: Methuen, 1989), 2. Duffy addresses the question of what constituted an "edition" for Methuen on p. 8.

58. Corelli, "My First Book," 252n, 246–47, 243.

59. A. Bennett, *Fame and Fiction: An Enquiry into Certain Popularities* (London: Grant Richards, 1901), 89.

60. Mumby and Norrie, *Publishers and Publishing*, 279.

61. Gettmann, *Victorian Publisher*, 89, 140–41. And it would appear that Marie Corelli herself arranged the distribution of "Song of Miriam" through Tillotson's Fiction Bureau in 1892. See Michael Turner, "Tillotson's Fiction Bureau: Agreements with Authors," *Studies in the Book Trade in Honour of Graham Pollard* (Oxford: Oxford Bibliographical Society, 1975), 372 n. 18.

62.   See *The Archives of Richard Bentley and Sons, 1829–1898* (Cambridge: Chadwyck-Healey, 1976), pt. 1, "Letterbooks, 1885–1892" 86:281–82, 385, 453, 301, 236; 88:78–79. I am grateful to Macmillan Publishers, Ltd., for permission to cite the Bentley Archives and to Chadwyck-Healey, Ltd., for permission to cite their edition of the Bentley Archives.

63.   Marie Corelli, *The Sorrows of Satan, or the Strange Experience of One Geoffrey Tempest, Millionaire* (London: Methuen, 1895), 1. All page references in the text are to this edition.

64.   "Literary Notes," *Pall Mall Gazette*, 5 October 1895, 3.

65.   W. T. Stead, "The Book of the Month: 'The Sorrows of Satan'—and of Marie Corelli," *Review of Reviews*, 12 (October 1895), 453.

66.   Michael Sadleir, "Mary Mackay," *DNB*, 1922–1930, 4th suppl., 540.

67.   Ibid., 540; *Athenaeum*, 5 October 1895, 438.

68.   *Clarion*, 12 October 1895, 323; *Pall Mall Gazette*, 18 October 1895, 4; 23 October 1895, 4; *Guardian*, 22 October 1895, 20. There were also announcements in the *Daily Chronicle*, 23 October 1895, 4, and the *Daily News*, 23 October 1895, 6.

69.   *Athenaeum*, 2 November 1895, 595; *Saturday Review*, 2 November 1895, 594; *Athenaeum*, 30 November 1895, 741; 14 December 1895, 823.

70.   Stead, "Book of the Month," 453.

71.   Sadleir, "Mary Mackay," 540.

72.   Masters, *Barabbas*, 143.

73.   W. L. Courtney, "Books of the Day," *Daily Telegraph*, 25 October 1895, 6.

74.   Bullock, *Corelli*, 118, 93; Bigland, *Corelli*, 148; Masters, *Barabbas*, 126.

75.   Corelli, "My First Book," 240, 242, 250.

76.   Here I am attempting to present a materialist account of the historical "accident" which Michael Sadleir noted: "It may be doubted if *The Sorrows of Satan* would have attained a popularity which broke all records, but for the accident of its date in publishing history. It was among the early books of fiction which appeared in a single six-shilling volume, and in consequence benefited to an incalculable degree from public excitement over the collapse of the three-decker." "Mary Mackay," 540.

77.   A. St. John Adcock, "Marie Corelli: A Record and an Appreciation," *Bookman*, 36 (May 1909), 60.

78.   H. J. Dyos, *Victorian Suburb: A Study of Camberwell* (Leicester: Leicester University Press, 1966), 25, 22.

79.   The *OED* citations suggest that the adjective is a slightly out-of-date (1879) Oxford/Cambridge slang word for "ostentatious."

80.   Gail Cunningham, *The New Woman and the Victorian Novel* (New York: Barnes and Noble, 1978), 10.

81.   Duffy, *Thousand Capricious Chances*, 44.

82. *The Literary Year-Book: 1897* (London: George Allen, 1897), 9.

83. Stead, "Book of the Month," 464.

84. E. A. B., "Music and Mummery: Sorrows of Satan," *Woman*, 20 January 1897, 9, 8. Bennett had read *The Sorrows of Satan* in October 1895, when he wrote to George Sturt, "I can now understand both her popularity & the critics' contempt." *Letters of Arnold Bennett*, ed. James Hepburn (London: Oxford University Press, 1966–1986), 2:24–25 n. 14.

85. "Barbara," "Book Chat: A Certain Miss Corelli," *Woman*, 4 August 1897, 8.

86. Bennett, "The Master-Christian," *Fame and Fiction*, 94, 83.

87. "Barbara," "Book Chat," *Woman*, 22 August 1894, 8.

88. "Barbara," "Book Chat: 'The Christian,'" *Woman*, 25 August 1897, 8, 9.

89. Bennett, "A Note on the Revolution in Journalism," *Fame and Fiction*, 125.

90. Arnold Bennett, "Mrs Humphrey Ward's Heroines," *Books and Persons: Being Comments on a Past Epoch, 1908–1911* (New York: George H. Doran, 1917), 47. While here I can only speculate, this innovation would seem to be determined by the change in the literary mode of production, i.e., "seasons," even "the Season," became swamped by the new, capitalist production of best-sellers.

91. Margaret Drabble, *Arnold Bennett* (New York: Knopf, 1974), 41–78. See also Arnold Bennett, *The Truth about an Author* (New York: George H. Doran, 1911), 21–113.

92. Quoted in Cynthia L. White, *Women's Magazines, 1693–1968* (London: Michael Joseph, 1970), 73.

93. Bennett, *Truth about an Author*, 32; Drabble, *Bennett*, 49.

94. James G. Nelson, *The Early Nineties: A View from the Bodley Head* (Cambridge: Harvard University Press, 1971), chap. 3, "Belles-Lettres to Sell"; James Hepburn, Introduction, *Letters of Arnold Bennett* 1:9–10; Ian Fletcher, "Decadence and the Little Magazine," in *Decadence and the 1890s*, ed. Fletcher (London: Arnold, 1979), 194.

95. Hepburn, Introduction, *Arnold Bennett: The Critical Heritage* (London: Routledge & Kegan Paul, 1981), 10, 5–8.

96. Introduction, *Wellesley Index* 2:xiii, and lists of contributors.

97. Bennett, *Truth about an Author*, 38.

98. *The Journal of Arnold Bennett, 1896–1928* (New York: Viking, 1933), 72–73.

99. Arnold Bennett, *How to Become an Author* (London: Pearson, 1903), 9–14, 17–18.

100. Bennett, *Truth about an Author*, 99–100.

101. Bennett, *Letters* 1:50.

102. Bennett, *Journal*, 83.

103. Nelson, *Early Nineties*, 36–45, 55.

104. R. D. Brown, "The Bodley Head Press: Some Bibliographical Extrapolations," *Papers of the Bibliographical Society of America*, 61 (1967), 41, 42, 40; see also A. J. A. Symons, "An Unacknowledged Movement in Fine Printing," in *Fleuron Anthology*, ed. F. Meynell and H. Simon (Toronto: University of Toronto Press, 1973), 308.

105. J. E. Morpungo, *Allen Lane: King Penguin* (London: Hutchinson, 1979), 21; Brown, "Bodley Head Press," 44, 42 n. 7:"From the earliest publications of the press, the advertising, the reviews, and the parodies stress the economic possibilities of collecting Bodley Head 'rare' editions."

106. Nelson, *Early Nineties*, 268, 106; Morpungo, *Allen Lane*, 25, 43.

107. Brown, "Bodley Head Press," 48.

108. Ibid., 48; Symons, "Unacknowledged Movement," 314; Wendell V. Harris, "John Lane's Keynote Series and the Fiction of the 1890s," *PMLA*, 83 (1968), 1407; Fletcher, "Decadence," 193, 192.

109. This account is drawn from Kathleen Lyon Mix, *A Study in Yellow: The Yellow Book and Its Contributors* (Lawrence: University of Kansas Press, 1960), 140–49; Brown says that there was "an almost complete turnover of the writers on Lane's list. In place of the Vanished Decadents are Grant Allen, Arnold Bennett, Herbert Flowerdew. . . ." "Bodley Head Press," 49 n. 19.

110. Bennett, *Truth about an Author*, 51; Hepburn, Introduction, *Letters* 1:12–13; *Letters* 2:15.

111. "Barbara," "Book Chat," *Woman*, 8 May 1895, 8.

112. Hepburn, Introduction, *Letters* 1:18.

113. Bennett, *Truth about an Author*, 73–76; Hepburn, Introduction, *Critical Heritage*, 13–14.

114. Bennett, *Truth about an Author*, 80.

115. E. A. B., "The Fallow Fields of Fiction," *Academy*, 60 (15 June 1901), 517.

116. Bennett, *Truth about an Author*, 63; E. A. Bennett, *A Man from the North* (London: John Lane, The Bodley Head, 1898), 231, 219. All page references in the text are to this edition.

117. Bennett, *Truth about an Author*, 64, 65.

118. *Academy*, 26 March 1898, Supplement, 348.

119. *Athenaeum*, 19 March 1898, 370.

120. Eden Philpotts, "'Black and White,' March, 1898," in *Critical Heritage*, 144.

121. Bennett, *Journal*, 49, 87, 88.

122. E. A. B., "The Fallow Fields of Fiction-III," *Academy*, 61 (20 July 1901), 58.

123. Drabble, *Bennett*, 67.

124. "Sarah Volatile," "Books and Authors," *Hearth and Home*, 3 March 1898, in *Critical Heritage*, 139.

125. Bennett, *Truth about an Author*, 110.

126. H. G. Wells, *Experiment in Autobiography* (Toronto: Macmillan, 1934), 534, 535.

Index